DARK DAMES, DASTARDLY DEEDS

DARK DAMES, DASTARDLY DEEDS

Women Who Chose to 'Cross the Line'

William J. Allender

NH

NEW
HOLLAND

First published in 2022 by New Holland Publishers
Sydney • Auckland

Level 1, 178 Fox Valley Road, Wahroonga, NSW 2076, Australia
5/39 Woodside Ave, Northcote, Auckland 0627, New Zealand

newhollandpublishers.com

A record of this book is held at the National Library of Australia.

ISBN 9781760794408

Group Managing Director: Fiona Schultz
Publisher: Lesley Pagett
Project Editor: Liz Hardy
Designer: Andrew Davies
Production Director: Arlene Gippert

10 9 8 7 6 5 4 3 2 1

Keep up with New Holland Publishers:
NewHollandPublishers
@newhollandpublishers

Contents

	Introduction	7
1.	A Life for a Life: Ruth Ellis	9
2.	The Self-Made Widow: Nannie Doss	31
3.	Dancing with Death: Yvonne Fletcher	41
4.	Pastries and Poison: Caroline Grills	53
5.	Rats and Rugby: The Veronica Monty Case	57
6.	Mum the Murderer: Diane Downs	65
7.	The Drowning Tub Murders: Andrea Yates	71
8.	Death in a Duck Pond: The Rachel Pfitzner Case	77
9.	Mothers and Methadone: A Deadly 'Sedative'	83
10.	Death of Innocence: The Kristi Anne Abrahams Case	97
11.	The 'Black Widow': The Kerry Forrest Case	103
12.	The Aberdeen Butcher: The Katherine Knight Case	113
13.	Psychosis and a Case of Patricide: Shamin Fernando	129
14.	Death House Landlady: Dorothea Puente	137
15.	The Sex Toy Strangler: Jamie Lee Dolheguy	145
16.	The Ward Four Killer: Beverley Gail Allitt	151
17.	Murder in a Heartbeat: Kristen Heather Gilbert	159
18.	Murder by Insulin: The Megan Haines Case	165
19.	The Curry Killing: Lakhvir Kaur Singh	177
20.	The Ice Cream Killer: Estibaliz Carranza	185
	Acknowledgements	193
	References & Further Reading	195

'There is no fouler fiend than a woman when her mind is bent on evil.'
– Homer

Dedicated to
the victims of the crimes
and their long-suffering families.

INTRODUCTION

It is yet another hot, steamy summer day in Sydney, Australia with the humidity approaching the mid-nineties and there is a hint of an afternoon thunderstorm. A cloaked barrister blots the sweat off his brow as he strides into the courtroom, one of the many participants in yet another human drama. We all have secrets, some more than others, in the dark side of human nature. But murder, to intentionally take a human life, is one of the gravest crimes one could commit.

What brings people to kill? What goes through their minds? Not being a psychologist, even with the cases where I've provided testimony in court, I have found it difficult to comprehend why some people have found in necessary to end the life of a person. In most cases, and certainly in my experience, the perpetrator of the crime is male. But, here is a selection of case stories (some names have been changed for legal reasons), from the many I have been involved in over the years where the villain was actually *female*. Yes, the evil female criminals (femmes fatales) who carried out their dastardly deeds on the unfortunate victims. Generally, the victims have been their spouses and/or lovers, but sometimes other family members. Sometimes, mental illness may have played a role in the crimes.

Also, included are some other stories I was not involved with, but which will, hopefully, illustrate how the dark forces, if not constrained, can dominate their victims and if not take their life, can ruin it in many other ways.

I hope you find them both interesting and informative.

Dr William J. Allender
Forensic scientist
MSc; PhD; FRACI; FACBS

1.

A LIFE FOR A LIFE:
RUTH ELLIS

'Heaven has no rage like love to hatred turned,
nor hell a fury like a woman scorned.'
– William Congreve

David Blakely and Ruth Ellis.

This is an infamous murder case which involved a very attractive woman by the name of Ruth Ellis. Ruth was attracted to a handsome, much younger man by the name of David Blakely, who enjoyed the dangerous and thrilling sport of car racing. It was a tumultuous affair, which sadly resulted in a double tragedy.

■

This story begins in Hampstead, a delightful village suburb located 6.4 kilometres (4 miles) north of the centre of London. It is considered one of the most genteel of the capital's suburbs, known for its liberal, artistic, musical and literary associations, along with its traditional pubs and eclectic mix of restaurants. In addition, it has some of the most expensive housing in London. A very affluent area.

It was in this setting that this tragic story unfolds.

It was a busy evening at the Little Club in Brompton Road, Kensington where Ruth's problems first began. It was here she met Desmond Cussen, a wealthy businessman, who was infatuated with her. Sadly, the feelings were not reciprocated to the same extent, although she was fond of him and called upon him whenever she found herself in difficulty. The ever-patient man rarely let her down. David Blakely entered the scene, further complicating the relationship. Blakely had earlier consumed an unknown number of drinks with some friends and was quite drunk when he turned up at the bar that evening, just before Christmas in 1953. He cruised the room leering at the women and turned to his friends saying, 'I suppose these are the so-called hostesses?'

Ruth Ellis was seated at the bar and was not impressed by the comment. However, she did notice that he was boyish, good looking, and while dressed in a well-worn tweed jacket and baggy grey flannel trousers, he appeared to have no shortage of cash, ordering double gins for the house, some 15 drinks all up. Nice.

Ruth turned to one of the club regulars and asked, 'Who's that guy?'

'Oh, that's David Blakely. He's a racingcar driver,' he answered.

Then Blakely briefly turned his attention to Ruth asking, 'I suppose you are another of them?'

'No, as a matter of fact I'm an old has-been,' she retorted.

This was quite an extraordinary comment as Ruth was anything but a 'has-been'. Her 27th birthday was only a couple of weeks away and she was quite a striking young woman. Ruth's pale complexion contrasted sharply with her bright red lips and her peroxide bleached blonde hair.

She was in reality, quite a stunner.

But she had also 'been around' as she once said to her elder sister, 'You may be my older sister, but I'm ten bloody years older than you in experience.'

Blakely appeared not to notice her reply as he downed his final double gin. The excessive drink consumption was probably now having its effects, as he threw an unprovoked punch at Desmond Cussen, Ruth's nearby companion, and was subsequently asked to leave.

'Alright, come on boys, let's get out of this den of iniquity.'

As David Blakely and his companions departed, Ruth Ellis spun around on her bar stool and said to the barmaid and well within earshot of patrons, 'I hope never to set eyes on that little shit again.'

But, unfortunately for all parties concerned, he did return. Along with a bunch of roses and belated apologies. Ruth then changed her mind about David Blakely and, amazingly, they eventually became lovers.

This tale was about to become a drama of passion with a deadly ending.

Ruth was born on 9 October 1926, the second daughter and fourth child of Bertha and Arthur Hornby in Rhyl, north Wales. Her father was a musician, believed to be an accomplished cellist, and he went under the stage name of Neilson. Hence, her initial full name was Ruth Hornby Neilson. Rhyl is a Welsh seaside resort town west of Liverpool in England, the great port from where cruise ships and liners crossed the Atlantic Ocean and the Mediterranean. The ships all had orchestras or bands to entertain the passengers and for much of Ruth's early life, her father was away at sea. It was a tough call for Bertha who was left to raise the children, but with four children to be fed, clothed and educated sacrifices had to be made. Even so, Bertha still managed to join her husband from time to time, leaving friends to take care of the children. However, the work was erratic and not reliable.

In 1933, the family left Rhyl for Basingstoke, south-west of London, where Arthur Neilson took up a position as a musician playing at a movie theatre. He hated the job which he thought was beneath his capabilities. But with the birth of two more daughters and a decline in the cruise ship business due to the Depression of the 1930s, he had little choice but to take it on. Unfortunately, he vented his frustrations on his family members which left lasting impressions on his children, including his then little daughter, Ruth.

Unfortunately, things got worse when he lost his movie theatre job. The 'talkies' were now replacing the silent films. The musicians who supported the silent films were no longer needed. Such is progress.

Consequently, Neilson moved his family to Southwark in south London to take up a job as a chauffeur. Ruth was only 14 when she left school and took up a job as a waitress at a modest restaurant. It was during the 1940s Blitz, a tough time for many UK residents, especially Londoners. The restaurant was often packed with servicemen who were ready to flirt with the waitresses before going into battle. It didn't take Ruth long to realise that generous tips were to be had for a girl who flirted back. In addition, she took to heart the saying 'gentlemen prefer blondes' (some years later a screen siren, Marilyn Monroe, adopted the same policy). Ruth bleached her hair with peroxide until it was a gleaming platinum blonde.

The 'ugly duckling' had now become a seductive 'swan'.

One night, tragedy struck when a bomb levelled their apartment house trapping her father Arthur Neilson in the rubble. Ruth arrived home shortly after it happened, and courageously helped to free him from the wreckage of the house. He had suffered severe head injuries which left him unable to hold down a full-time job for the rest of his life. Ruth's brothers were in the British Army and fighting abroad against the German military.

To supplement the family income, Ruth, along with her sister, Muriel, took up employment at a nearby munitions factory. (There is some difference here in the reports as to whether the sisters were employed by a munitions or an Oxo factory. I guess, both helped the war effort whether it was the supply of bullets to take enemy life or supply food to sustain allied life.)

The fast and harried romantic life Ruth had taken on no doubt contributed to her health suffering. It was during this time she contracted rheumatic fever and was treated at St Giles Hospital in Camberwell. It could have been worse.

On her recuperation, she took up dancing to improve her fitness and also took up elocution lessons to improve her social confidence.

In the autumn of 1943, the now 16-year-old Ruth, while working as a dance hall photographer's assistant,, met a Canadian soldier, Private Clare. He was a French-Canadian soldier about ten years older than she. In his uniform, and with his dark good looks, he was a strikingly handsome young man. The teenage Ruth was smitten.

Private Clare introduced Ruth to the glitzy West End district of London, wooing her with fresh flowers, especially red carnations, and bottles of champagne. It was in the new year of 1944 that Ruth realised that she had become pregnant to him. She had just turned 17.

Private Clare offered to marry her, but Bertha Neilson wrote to his commanding officer to check on his background. Sadly, it was revealed that Clare was married and had a wife and children in Canada.

Ruth's son, Clare Andrea Neilson, was born on 15 September 1944 and so she, her mother and elder sister Muriel were left literally holding the baby. For a time, the father helped support his infant son. Then in 1945, a letter and a bouquet of two-dozen red roses arrived at the Neilson residence. It was the last Ruth heard from Private Clare.

It was a very tough time for Ruth, deserted by the man she loved and now left with the responsibility of raising a child. It was some years later that Ruth's mother would wistfully remark: 'I shall always think Ruth's life would have turned out differently, if the child's father had been able to marry her.'

In 1946, with additional responsibilities, including a child and now partially disabled parents, Ruth had to get a stable, well-paid job. She saw an advertisement for evening work: 'Wanted. Model for Camera Club. Nude but artistic poses. No experience required. Highest references available. Confidential.'

Essentially, the job entailed posing nude for fee-paying 'amateur photographers'. It was all very grubby really, but the pay was a pound per hour. In just three hours, she could earn more than her 44-hour stint at the factory. After work, members often took her to dinner and dancing in the West End of London, where Clare had taken her earlier. It was here she was seen by Morris Conley, the owner of the Court Club. He recognised Ruth's potential and was keen to have her join his staff. Conley promptly offered her a job as a hostess. It was an offer she could not refuse. It was a step up from nude modelling and, not unsurprisingly, she accepted the offer.

It was very good money for the time, starting at a base salary of five pounds per week. In addition, Ruth was paid 10 per cent commission on the food and drink her customers bought. Under Conley's guidance, she soon was able to triple her five-pound base pay with bar commissions – and more, depending what customers paid for her sexual services. Sex was one of the additional services provided at the Court Club. Of course, the business owner Morris Conley took his percentage of the proceeds from his hostesses.

Ruth soon became the envy of the other hostesses and was considered an 'artist' in her skilled lovemaking but, curiously, would be very offended if she was described as a prostitute. To her mind, her customers were friends she came to know within the club precinct. In Ruth's view, she was an 'enterprising modern woman.'

After another unwanted pregnancy in 1950, followed by a quickly arranged abortion, Ruth, now 23 years old, no doubt started to think about her son, Andrea and their future. One of her customers appeared to provide a solution for domestic stability that Ruth craved. He was George Johnson Ellis, a recently divorced 41-year-old dentist with a practice in Surrey. Here was a wealthy, professional man, educated, cultivated and from a good family background. And he was totally besotted by Ruth. A very promising candidate.

Further, he confided to Ruth that he expected a substantial inheritance when his almost 70-year-old mother had died.

Unfortunately, George turned out to be a very heavy drinker.

They seemed an inappropriate couple, the florid, balding, middle-aged man and the young, platinum-blonde woman. However, she said to her sister, Muriel: 'I do respect him and love him. It really is the real thing.'

In September 1950, Ruth moved into Ellis's home in Sanderstead with her now six-year-old son. Her mission was to marry him, persuade him to stop drinking, and to take her position in society as a respectable wife and mother. Eventually, on Ruth's insistence, Ellis checked into Warlingham Park Hospital to treat his alcoholism. After spending several weeks in the facility, he emerged declaring himself cured.

Ruth was overjoyed.

On 8 November 1950, they were married in a private ceremony at the Registrar's Office in the town of Tonbridge. Unfortunately, the following day, George Ellis was drunk again. A week later, he was checking into Warlingham Park Hospital again. This became a regular pattern of behaviour. Out again, cured again, drunk again, checking in again. The man truly had a problem!

The situation became increasingly tense when Ruth found that she was pregnant again, barely two months after the wedding. Rather than being a joyous event, her advancing pregnancy only seemed to make things worse – and nastier in the Ellis household.

On 2 October, 1951 Ruth Ellis gave birth to a daughter, with her devoted sister by her side. The baby was named Georgina after her husband, but he wanted nothing to do with the child. In November, only a year after they married, George Ellis filed for divorce on the grounds of mental cruelty. Ruth did not contest the petition. She had apparently had enough.

Under British law, it would be three years before the divorce became final. Ruth Ellis now had two children to support.

In December 1951 she sought out her old job in the West End with Morris Conley, leaving Andria (now known as 'Andy') and Georgina in the care of her family. Her former boss welcomed her back enthusiastically and to top off her return, Conely provided her with a two-bedroom apartment, rent free. While modest, it was located in Mayfair, an elegant suburb. This address meant a great deal to Ruth. She had now achieved the status she craved.

In the meantime, the Court Club had been upgraded with a restaurant and dance floor being installed and was now known as the Carroll Club.

For the next year or so, Ruth was truly in her favoured environment.

It was probably, one of the happiest periods of her life. The men adored her and her friendships included many from the moneyed and married international set.

Yes, she had arrived.

After a brief health fright in December 1952, Ruth was back at Carroll's touting her various skills with gusto. The following summer and autumn of 1953 were very prosperous for the now 26-year-old Ruth Ellis. So much so, she was able to ease off pushing the expensive dubious drinks and party when she pleased.

It was April, 1953 and times were changing. A new crowd was emerging for her to make friends with as the racing-car-driver fraternity sought a new after-hours outlet. They moved from their favourite hangout, the Steering Wheel Club, after it closed at 11 pm, to one which stayed open until 3 am, the Carroll Club. The group was led by charismatic Mike Hawthorne, a tall, blond 23-year-old who was on his way to becoming a world racing-car champion. And David Blakely was among those who basked in Hawthorne's reflected glory.

David Moffat Drummond Blakely was born on 17 June 1929, the youngest of John and Annie's four children. They were a typical English upper-middle-class family and David Blakely's father Dr John was a much respected general practitioner in Sheffield, a steel town in northern England, where he carried out his practice. And while nannies took care of the children and servants took care of their luxurious Tudor home, Annie organised charity bazaars and social ventures. It was an idyllic life.

However, on a chilly evening in 1934, everything started to fall apart. A 25-year-old woman named Phyllis Stanton was dropped at her parents' place almost dead from acute septicaemia (a blood poisoning condition). Before Ms Stanton died the following day, she told her parents that Dr John had brought her home. Further investigation revealed that she had contracted the fatal infection due to a botched abortion.

Dr John Blakely was subsequently charged with murder. An inquest was held to determine the events that led up to Ms Phyllis Stanton's death. Dr Blakely admitted that he had an affair with Ms Stanton but said he was only one of many lovers. He also said that on learning she was pregnant, he had supplied a drug to her to induce an abortion, but denied carrying out any operation on her.

The prosecution felt they had little evidence to charge him and in the end the Sheffield magistrates dismissed all charges. Dr Blakely's practice still survived, but his marriage suffered. His wife never forgave him for his infidelity and after six years of domestic arguments and upheaval, Annie Blakely finally divorced Dr John Blakely in 1940 on the grounds of adultery. Custody of the children went to the mother.

In 1941 Annie remarried to Humphrey Wyndam Cook who was, in his youth, one of Britain's well-known race-car drivers. And he was very wealthy to boot. Cook took 11-year-old David under his wing and introduced him to the world of racing cars. At every opportunity, David skipped his studies at school to pore over various racing-car journals. During school vacations, he and his stepfather would attend as many racing-car meetings as possible. After a brief stint with the military, David's mother and stepfather purchased a comfortable apartment near their home and arranged for his nanny to take care of him. In addition, Cook used his many connections to get several jobs for his stepson. Unfortunately, David Blakely wasn't interested in a regular job or, indeed, working. What he wanted most in life was to tinker with race cars and hang out with the racing-car crowd at the Steering Wheel Club, getting drunk in the process.

David's passion was to become a professional racing-car driver. And this passion was further stimulated when his stepfather bought him a second-hand H. R. Godfrey (H.R.G) sports car for his birthday. He aspired to be a professional, but he never really made it past amateur level. He was, by all accounts, adequate technically. However, he apparently lacked a first-rate driver's stamina and, more importantly, the courage to really push himself to the next level.

In 1951 David Blakely met up with Anthony ('Ant') Findlater who had advertised an antique Alfa Romeo for sale. He didn't go ahead with the purchase but invited Findlater around to look at his H.R.G. sports car. The two hit it off and struck a deal. Findlater agreed to keep the vehicle in top mechanical condition, while David would race it.

Unfortunately, Blakely not only wanted Findlater's mechanical expertise, he had taken a shine to his pretty, dark-haired wife, Carole. They subsequently had a brief affair that was soon dissolved. Amazingly, things were soon sorted and the Findlaters and David Blakely remained friends. Maybe it was their joint interest in cars that kept the bond between them intact!

In February 1952, David Blakely's biological father died from a heart attack, leaving 7000 pounds to each of his four children. It was a significant sum of money for the time and allowed David to behave as the 'big spender' as soon as the drinking clubs opened, from the Steering Wheel to the Little Club. Here he had enjoyable afternoons boozing and boasting about his racing exploits. Generally fictitious by most accounts. But his hosts seemed to enjoy a good yarn, not to mention the occasional free booze!

In the summer of 1953, David decided to use what was left of his inheritance to build and race a sports car. The sports car was given the moniker the 'Emperor'.

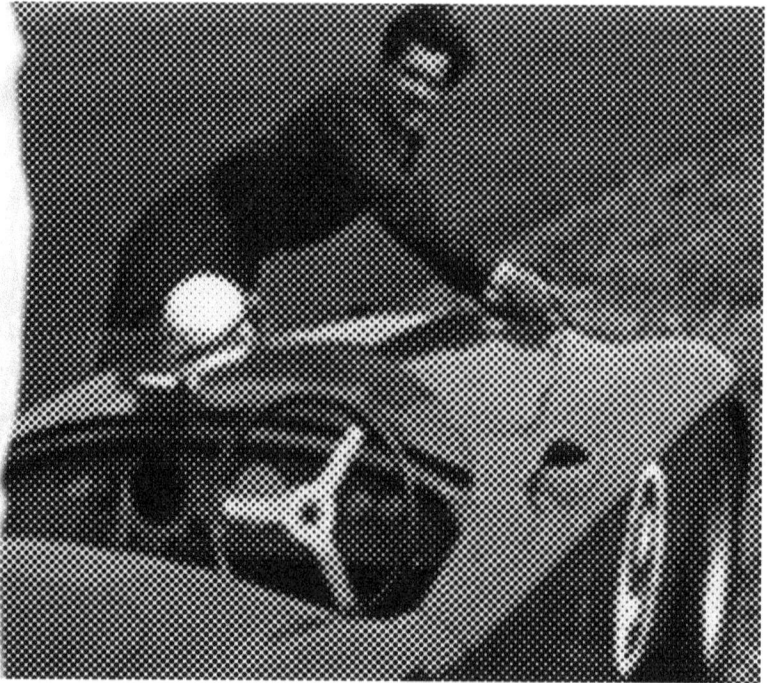

David Blakely with his beloved 'Emperor' race car.
PHOTOGRAPH COURTESY OF BBC NEWS, UK

David Blakely offered Anthony ('Ant') Findlater a salary of 10 pounds a week to look after the project. A garage space was leased and the H.R.G. body of the sports car was modified and a twin overhead–cam 1500 cc Singer–H.R.G. engine was installed to power the vehicle.

This was an expensive venture and Blakely turned to his stepfather for further capital.

Humphrey Cook was a decent, patient man. But when he got wind of David's numerous affairs, he was quite unhappy about them.

While he didn't cut off his allowance, he refused to pay for any expenses associated with the Emperor racing car. But David was quite a resourceful young man and knew how to get around his parents. On 11 November 1953 in *The Times* of London under 'Forthcoming Marriages' he placed an advertisement stating his engagement to a young woman by the name of Mary Dawson. Mary was 21 year old from a rich woollen-goods manufacturer in northern England and she was considered an ideal match for David by his parents. They were delighted with the engagement announcement and Humphrey Cook then approved the funds for servicing the Emperor.

However, Blakely had other plans and within two weeks of the engagement announcement, he had moved into a two-bedroom apartment over the Little Club, occupied rent free by Ruth Ellis. This was part of the deal Morris Conley offered Ruth to manage the Little Club. In addition, she was paid a salary of 15 pounds per week, along with a 10-pound weekly entertainment allowance to spend on customers. In the first few months of their relationship, Ruth was still able to manage the Little Club and her finances effectively. While leaving her nights for David, she entertained customers during the afternoons when he was away. By early 1954 Ruth was pregnant again, most likely by Blakely, who had been living with her for about four months. But in reality, it could have been any one of her male clients. According to Ruth, David then offered to marry her. However, this would have been tricky, as Ruth was still officially married to George Ellis and David Blakely was engaged to Mary Dawson. In any case, Ruth had an abortion, paid for by Desmond Cussen.

But the year still had more misery in store for Ruth Ellis.

A trip to the race track proved to be a social disaster. Blakely had neglected to tell her of the dress code for the track meet. Unfortunately, Ruth dressed more appropriately for a cocktail party and was shocked to be shunned by the other women at the event. Being an adaptable woman, she then concentrated her attentions on the men there who thought she was 'tremendous fun'. Fair enough.

But Blakely wasn't impressed and it was a very tense trip back to London for the pair.

As time went on, David Blakely became increasingly concerned about Ruth's free and easy relationships with the men at the club. He was aware that she entertained other men at the apartment and was heard to say, 'It's not what you do at night that worries me. It's what you do in the afternoon.'

Ruth also began to have concerns about her lover.

The supposedly wealthy Blakely cadged drinks from her and other customers. But, more of concern was his resultant drunken behaviour that caused trouble and upset customers, affecting business at the club. Not to mention his flirting with the female customers.

Well, what was 'good for the goose was good for the gander', as the saying goes!

Further, there was the additional problem of Ruth's boss, Morris Conley. He knew David Blakely was now living in the apartment with Ruth. He wasn't happy and starting charging her rent. An unwelcome extra expense.

While Ruth recognised the risks David Blakely was causing to her livelihood, she was an astute manager. But she found it difficult, if not impossible, to end the passionate affair.

In June 1954, Blakely went to France with the Findlaters to take part in the gruelling 24-hour Le Mans competition. David was to be the relief driver for the Bristol Works team. He was ecstatic, at last a true racing-car driver. And as relief driver in a world-class competition. It truly was a highlight of his life, even though his vehicle was unplaced.

He mailed Ruth a postcard which said, *'Arrived O.K. Haven't had a drink for three days!!! Wish you were here. Will probably see you Tuesday.*

Love David.'

Ruth was delighted and organised a party at the Little Club to celebrate David's 25th birthday and his team's efforts at Le Mans for Thursday 17 June. Sadly, the day came and went without Blakely showing up. Not surprisingly, Ruth Ellis was very disappointed and deeply upset.

She then turned her attentions to Desmond Cussen and for the first time the two become lovers. She declared to her long-faithful suitor, 'I'm not married to David and I can lead my own life.'

On Blakely's return, Ruth, curiously, still allowed David Blakely to sleep with her.

But the arguments continued. It was the beginning of, if not already, a very unstable relationship.

Eventually, the tensions between the pair began to impact upon business at the Little Club.

Ruth tried to boost business by flirting with the remaining customers, which only further enraged Blakely. Further, she refused to end her relationship with Desmond Cussen. And why should she? He was a devoted benefactor and even paid for her now 10-year-old son Andy to attend an expensive boarding school.

But worse, aside from the jealousies experienced, alcohol and drugs had also crept into the relationship. Ruth had been a regular drinker for years, but now she was drinking more than ever, consuming as much as a bottle of Pernod a day. (Pernod is an unsweetened aniseed liqueur first made in 1805 by Henri-Louis Pernod that is often enjoyed during meals as a digestive. It is quite potent, containing 40% alcohol, comparable to Scotch, vodka and whisky.) In addition, she was taking a sedative that had been prescribed to her during her problems with George Ellis. And Blakely had started taking amphetamines ('speed'), no doubt picked up from the various track meets he attended.

It was like pouring petrol (gasoline) onto a fire.

One patron allegedly said, 'They were so violently passionate with each other that any sort of control disappeared.'

In their sexual encounters, David would be under the influence of speed and grog alcohol. While Ruth was stoned from the effects of her sedative and Pernod. They also inhaled amyl nitrite, a potent vasodilator, which kept them coupling, lusting and fighting for hours.

It was truly a prescription for disaster.

Eventually, Morris Conley could not take anymore. The months of declining profits and bad behaviour from his star manager and her errant lover were too much. In December 1954 Ruth Ellis and Morris Conley jointly decided that she should vacate the apartment and leave the 'Little'.

It was a sad day for both parties.

But again the devoted Desmond Cussen came to her rescue. He offered accommodation for Ruth and her son Andy in his apartment at Goodwood Court, in the affluent area of Marylebone. But the deal was conditional: Ruth was to stop seeing Blakely.

Sadly, she couldn't help herself and gave in to Blakely's antics of drinking heavily, followed by remorse and tearful pleading and finally a bouquet of red carnations.

The ever-patient Cussen then decided to pay for a one-bedroom apartment at 44 Egerton Gardens, Kensington for Ruth and her son. By February 1955, Blakely had also moved in, passing themselves off as a married couple. It wasn't long before Ruth found she was pregnant again and announced the news to David.

Blakely wasn't pleased with the announcement and greeted the news with violence, which included grabbing her by the throat and punching her in the stomach. Several days later Ruth miscarried.

Then on 31 March, still bleeding and recovering from the miscarriage, Ruth bravely made a 200-mile trip (about 322 kilometres) with Blakely for a race in which the Emperor race car was entered. Unfortunately, during a practice run the car broke down and Blakely angrily turned on Ruth blaming her for the mishap! Yes, he truly was a top bloke!

On Sunday 3 April, Ruth returned to Egerton Gardens and went to bed with a high fever. She was one sick woman. Fortunately, her son Andy was there to comfort her. Desmond Cussen had gone to the boy's boarding school to pick him up. It was an awful couple of days, where a desperately unhappy Ruth Ellis waited for a call and/or a visit from David Blakely.

Sadly, none came.

Then, on Wednesday 6 April, there was a turn of events. Ruth was recovering from her sickness and Blakely had just landed a job as assistant on the Bristol Works team that was aiming to be present in the Le Mans race in June that year. David was also photographed on the job. He was elated. In addition, he sent his now signature bouquet of red carnations by way of apology.

Further, on the following Thursday 7 April, he brought Ruth a photograph of himself with the inscription: 'To Ruth, with all my love. David.' Ruth was delighted and they spent a very pleasant evening together, followed by an intimate breakfast. He reportedly proposed to her, sealing her happiness.

However, it was to be their last time together.

The following Friday, Blakely had lunch at the Magdala Tavern with the Findlaters. It was here, where he revealed his true feelings. He was desperately unhappy and wanted to get away from Ruth 'I'm supposed to be calling Ruth at eight tonight,' he reportedly said, 'I can't stand it any longer, I want to get away from her.'

Carol Findlater asked why he didn't just leave her.

He apparently replied, 'It's not as easy as that. You don't know her. You don't know what she is capable of.' However, Anthony 'Ant' Findlater did, as he had seen Ruth's fury, and he allowed Blakely to stay with them at Tanza Road, Hampstead. Apparently, the agreed meeting was in fact 7.30 pm and Ruth had been waiting until 9.30 pm. Understandably, she was concerned and rang the Findlaters and asked to speak to David. She was told that Blakely wasn't there.

Over the next several hours Ruth rang the Findlaters and also rang Desmond Cussen requesting a lift. By now when Ant Findlater heard her voice on the phone he simply hung up. Even though it was now quite late, Cussen drove her to 29 Tanza Road. On reaching the destination, Ruth knew Blakely was there, as his grey Vanguard wagon was parked outside the Findlaters' apartment. She rang the doorbell and knocked on the front door. No-one answered, although a female giggle was heard from an open window.

Ruth was by now livid with rage. She took a large flashlight from

Desmond Cussen's glovebox and ran over to Blakely's wagon and smashed in the rear windows.

The lights of the apartment were now on, and Ant Findlater, in pyjamas and night robe, came down the stairs. Ruth demanded to see David. Findlater then reiterated that he was not there. While they were arguing, a police car pulled up – Findlater had called them earlier.

Unwilling to get involved in 'just another domestic' the police left after asking Cussen to take the agitated, humiliated woman home.

Frustrated, Ruth subsequently left with Desmond Cussen.

She reportedly said, 'I did not sleep that night. I just sat and howled. I no longer thought of David as the man I loved, but as someone who was trying to make a fool of me. I felt humiliated and frustrated.'

Sadly, it appears the subsequent events might have been prevented. As Ruth Ellis reflected sometime later, 'If only I had been able to speak to him and give vent to my feelings. I do not think any of this would have happened.'

At 8 am the next morning, she again phoned the Findlaters, but again the phone was hung up on her. They clearly did not want to answer any of her calls.

In frustration, Ruth again asked Desmond Cussen to take her to 29 Tanza Road, Hampstead. Ruth told Desmond that she was certain that David was having an affair with the Findlaters' young nanny saying, 'He's up to his old tricks again.'

On arriving at the Findlaters' address, she heard David's voice and another female's giggle. She was enraged.

She was now convinced that David was having an affair with the nanny. It was a very ironic situation, given they *both* had affairs.

Back at her apartment at 44 Egerton Gardens, Ruth had a restless night, smoking cigarettes, drinking Pernod and shaking with anger, she reviewed her life up to this sad point, 'When I first fell in love with David, I was a successful manageress of a prosperous club. I had admirers, money in the bank and a lovely flat. Now all I have is a bed-sitting room, no money, no job. A man who beat me in private and abused me in public. A man who was relieved when I lost the child he had fathered. I have a peculiar desire to kill David.'

On Easter Sunday evening, Desmond Cussen again drove Ruth Ellis to Penn to search for Blakely, where he worked for Silicon Pistons. Failing to find him they went back to London, where she waited for him outside the Findlaters' apartment. However, Blakely's now repaired Vanguard wagon was nowhere in sight and was later found at his other favourite drinking hole, the Magdala Tavern.

And there she found him. The Vanguard wagon was parked nearby. At last.

Ruth reached into her handbag and pulled out a pair of thick-lensed spectacles to look into the tavern. There she saw David Blakely, accompanied by Clive Gunnell (a mutual friend of Anthony Findlater), enjoying gin and tonics.

It was the last drink David Blakely was to enjoy.

Now seeing her quarry, Ruth put her eyeglasses back in her handbag and took out a long-barrelled .38 calibre Smith & Wesson revolver loaded with six nickel plated bullets. As she waited, David stumbled from the tavern, carrying a quart of beer and probably, due to the effects of the alcohol, was fumbling with his car keys. Following behind him was Clive Gunnell with two bottles of beer.

She aimed the revolver at Blakely, and called, 'David' as he turned to get into his Vanguard wagon.

He ignored her, or maybe he just didn't hear her call the first time.

She called again, 'David, David!'

This time he turned and faced her and was terrified at what he saw. It was an outstretched .38 and he was within its sights. He started to run. Ruth Ellis then fired off the first round, the bullet entering his lower right back, penetrating his liver and abdomen before exiting below his left shoulder blade. Blakely fell against the Vanguard, smearing the side panels with blood while crying out, 'Clive, Clive!'

'Get out of the way, Clive,' Ruth ordered, as she followed Blakely around the wagon.

He lurched down the street and collapsed into a gutter, with blood flowing from his mouth. Ruth then stood over him and pumped a further three more slugs into his twitching body.

She intended to also take her own life with the remaining bullets, but hesitated and as she lowered the revolver, a bullet was discharged, ricocheting off the footpath and unfortunately injuring a nearby bystander.

An off-duty police officer, Constable Alan Thompson, who was at the Magdala Tavern, arrested Ruth Ellis while she was still holding the weapon. At about midnight on 10 April, after a formal interview, she was charged with the wilful murder of David Blakely.

David Blakely was declared dead on arrival at the hospital. A subsequent post-mortem showed that of the four bullets that had entered his body, two had only caused superficial wounds. In addition to the first serious injury from the first bullet, the second bullet had penetrated his left lung, aorta and windpipe before lodging in the muscles of his tongue. The pathologist put the cause of death to be due to 'shock and haemorrhage due to gunshot wounds.'

Ruth Ellis was remanded to Holloway Prison to stand trial for murder.

During her stay, she requested a photograph of David Blakely and a Bible. The photograph was attached to the wall of her cell and the Bible opened to Deuteronomy 19:21 'And thine eye shall not pity; but life shall go for life, eye for eye, tooth for tooth, hand for hand, [and] foot for foot.'

An extraordinary woman.

However, after her initial interview on the Monday afternoon, Ms Ellis was examined by several doctors to determine her mental health to stand trial. These examinations were necessary under British law to ensure she was legally sane and therefore fit to plead at her trial. None of the doctors could find any evidence of mental illness and so the trial proceeded.

In addition, Mr John Bickford, an experienced criminal lawyer, was hired by the Mirror group of newspapers to represent her. He was quite frustrated at her lack of willingness to assist in her defence. She reportedly said, 'I took David's life and I don't ask that you save mine.' Adding, 'I don't want to live.'

(Unfortunately, the issue of how Ruth obtained the Smith & Wesson revolver and how she was shown how to shoot it was not raised. Indeed, it was suppressed by Ruth in her discussion with John Bickford. It seems likely that Desmond Cussen supplied the revolver on Ruth's request.

He simply gave in, as he had done for her time and time again. And most likely, also showed her how to use it.)

Ruth's parents, Arthur and Bertha Neilson regularly visited their daughter in the condemned cell. Her mother clearly concerned as to how things were proceeding, begged her to her to plead insanity. However, Ruth replied, 'It's no use, mother. I was sane when I did it and I meant to do it, and I won't go to prison for ten years or more, and come out old and finished.'

(The insanity plea would have been quite pointless, as Ruth had already been assessed by medical personnel during her incarceration.)

Sadly, Ruth Ellis appears to have been quite vain about her appearance, to her eventual detriment. As the trial date approached, she was beginning to get concerned about her appearance, with the brown roots of her hair beginning to show. The Holloway Governor Dr Charity Taylor allowed her to send out for the necessary materials to bleach her hair and generally spruce up her appearance. It was not a good strategy for Ruth.

John Bickford and other members of the defence team were dismayed. They hoped to present Ruth as a physically abused victim of a violent lover. It wasn't to be.

The matter went to trial and the case, not unexpectedly, had attracted a great deal of media attention and so drew very large crowds. Ruth Ellis's trial opened on Monday 20 June 1955 in the Old Bailey's Number One Court before Mr Justice Havers. The prosecution was led by Mr Christmas Humphries, assisted by Mr Mervyn Jones and Ms Jean Southworth. The defence was led by Mr Aubrey Stevenson, assisted by Mr Sebag Shaw and Mr Peter Rawlinson. The court on the day was jam packed.

On the opening day, when Ruth Ellis entered the Old Bailey courtroom, number one, her appearance was quite extraordinary. Her hair was now a glorious platinum sheen, and she was wearing a modish black suit with a lamb collar, a white silk blouse and stylish black high-heeled shoes. She looked more like a movie star than a defendant in a murder trial!

Ruth pleaded not guilty, apparently so her side of the situation could be told. However, the evidence of the killing was overwhelming.

But, she never expected an acquittal, and was keen to show the involvement of the Findlaters in an alleged plan to keep David away from her. (She never knew that David was part of the 'conspiracy 'or indeed, even instigated it!)

The trial only took about a day and a half, with John Bickford and his colleagues briefly cross-examining the Findlaters and the other prosecution witnesses presented. Given the evidence, the prosecution rested its case before the lunch recess.

Ruth Ellis took the stand that afternoon. Her defence lawyers did their best to depict her as jealous woman who was provoked well beyond reason to murder her lover. She was asked about the treatment she received by Blakely, namely the beatings she received.

She testified that, 'He [David] only hit me with his fist or hands. I bruise very easily, and I was full of bruises on many occasions.' She also described her miscarriage, 'A few weeks or days previously, I do not know which, and David got very violent. I do not know whether that caused the miscarriage or not. He thumped me in the tummy.'

Ruth was then asked by her defence attorneys why she killed David Blakely. She replied, 'I do not really know, quite seriously. I was just upset.'

The prosecution counsel Mr Christmas Humphreys then asked her, 'Mrs Ellis, when you fired that revolver at close range into the body of David Blakely what did you intend to do?'

Her answer was quite damaging, 'It was obvious that when I shot him I intended to kill him.' So the jury were now presented the admission that she carried out the shooting but, more importantly, it was an intent to kill.

But the defence did not give up and Mr Stevenson put to the court the issue of provocation. Mr Justice Havers said he had considered this issue, but ruled that there was 'insufficient material, even upon a view of the evidence most favourable to support a verdict of manslaughter on the grounds of provocation.' Essentially, the defence counsel's hands were now tied.

Ruth Ellis's fate was sealed.

At 10.30 am the following morning, the jury of 10 men and two women filed into the court where the judge instructed them that under British Law, 'transport of passion and loss of self-control' was not a defence for the charge of murder. It only took the jury 23 minutes to find Ruth Ellis guilty and there was no recommendation of mercy. It would have been hard for them to find any other verdict possible, given the evidence presented.

Mr Justice Havers had no other alternative but to sentence Ruth Ellis to her death. He then donned the traditional black cap as he condemned Ruth to death by hanging.

The execution was set down for Wednesday 13 July 1955. She was subsequently taken back to Holloway in a prison van and placed in the constantly lit and guarded condemned suite. Once the verdict was known, there were many attempts by anti-death penalty groups to have Ruth Ellis reprieved and to have her sentence commuted, with the Home Office receiving petitions containing several thousand signatures.

Despite the considerable public and media pressure, the Home Secretary ruled, '… If a reprieve were to be granted in this case, I think that we should have seriously to consider whether capital punishment should be retained as a penalty.' Also, in the police view, it was entirely Ruth Ellis's decision to shoot David Blakely. On 11 July, two days before her scheduled execution, her reprieve was denied with her file being marked, 'The Law Must Take Its Course'.

Like all prisoners, condemned or otherwise, Ruth was visited by various officials, as well as her family and friends. However, unbeknownst to Ruth, her trial solicitor, John Bickford, tried to make one final attempt to find out where she got the gun – and possibly get a reprieve. He sent an associate, Victor Mishcon, to see her in the condemned cell at 11.15 am on the Tuesday morning. He was astounded to see the woman in Holloway who was scheduled to be executed the next day. She was completely composed and greeted him by saying, 'How kind of you to come,' and behaved like a gracious hostess.

Ruth then opened up to Victor Mishcon saying, 'I am now completely composed. I know that I am going to die, and I'm ready to do so. You won't hear anything from me that says I didn't kill David. I did kill him. And whatever the circumstances you as a lawyer will appreciate that it's a life for a life. Isn't that just.'

He was struck by her calm demeanour. She then provided her version on how she got the gun and learnt how to use it.

Mischom took down the details and presented them in a statement for the Home Office in a last-minute quest for a reprieve.

Ruth Ellis signed the document. But it was too little, too late.

That evening, 12 July, her family visited her for the last time. She graciously asked her mother to place a dozen carnations, six white and six red, on David Blakely's grave. A curious sentimental payback.

It was a fine sunny morning when at 6.30 am on 13 July 1955 Ruth Ellis received Holy Communion from the prison chaplain. She didn't bother with breakfast, but eagerly accepted a glass of brandy before taking her place on the gallows floor. Albert Pierrepoint, the public executioner, placed a white hood over her head and then the loop of rope around her neck.

When all was in place, the trapdoor lever was pulled and Ruth Ellis was then flung into eternity. Mr Pierrepoint sometime later said that he had hanged some 430 people, 15 of whom were women, but Ruth Ellis was one of the bravest that ever stood before him.

Due to the huge outcry over this execution, and many protest demonstrations, Ruth Ellis became the last woman to be hanged in Britain.

Some good did come out of this tragedy, and the death penalty was subsequently abolished, but only ten years later.

I was somewhat saddened by this matter, as I felt Ruth Ellis had got a very raw deal out of the proceedings, given David Blakely's violent behaviour that she had been subjected to, which included grabbing her by the throat and, the worst, punching her in the stomach resulting in a miscarriage of their child – among many other misdemeanours.

Truly, a bad, very spoilt young man.

The next stories are quite different, and the intent was quite evil. These women truly crossed the line that separates good and evil.

2.

THE SELF-MADE WIDOW:
NANNIE DOSS

'Family, like arsenic, works best in small doses. Unless, you prefer to die.'
– David Levithan

A somewhat jovial Nannie (Nancy) Hazel Doss (c. 1955).

Nannie Doss was born Nancy Hazle on 4 November 1905 in the Blue Mountain, Alabama, and later adopted the name 'Nannie'. During her life she allegedly murdered four husbands, one in Alabama, one in North Carolina, one in Kansas and one in Oklahoma – the last one, Samuel Doss, for whose murder she was finally tried and convicted.

She is also alleged to have murdered her mother, two of her four daughters, a mother-in-law and other family members, by her favourite poison, arsenic trioxide, and giggled over it all, even during the police interviews!

■

Nancy or Nannie, the nickname she became known by, did not have a happy childhood. Life on the farm was hard, and quite often she had to stay home and help with the harvest rather than attending school, with her dad saying 'Into your calicos, and hurry down to the harvest'. As Nannie grew older, she liked to read the 'lonely hearts clubs' advertisements but her dad forbade any attendance to these 'sinful, fixed hair, hell-bent affairs'.

However, Nannie did manage to sneak away here and there to meet boys surreptitiously, and get a bit of loving herself, away from her father's eyes. The boys liked her: her eyes and hair were dark, her giggle bright, and she was easy, very easy. One of the boys she met was Charley Braggs, who was Nannie's besotted co-worker at the Linen Thread Company, where she went to work. Unlike the other boys, young Braggs was approved of by Nannie's father, James Hazle. Within four months after bringing the lad home one day for supper, Nannie found herself walking down the aisle to be married to Charley Braggs.

Some years later, Nannie wrote, 'I married, as my father wished, in 1921 to a boy I only knowed about four or five months who had no family, only a mother who was unwed and who had taken over my life completely when we were married. She never seen anything wrong with what he done, but she would take spells. She would not let my own mother stay all night …'

Unfortunately for Nannie, she did not lose a demanding father, but gained an even more demanding mother-in-law. Still, the Braggs family had four daughters within a four-year period, the first, Melvina in 1923, and the last, Florine in 1927. Tensions within the family increased – from raising babies, pleasing her mother-in-law, and being tied to the kitchen feeding a hungry family – and Nannie started drinking heavily, and her casual smoking habit became chronic.

The marriage had its ups and downs, which mostly became downs, and Nannie sought solace in the arms of strangers; as did her husband, who also found sexual satisfaction in other women. It became a curious relationship. Something of an open marriage and very unstable.

In early 1927, two of their middle daughters passed away. Each child had appeared okay at breakfast but died by lunchtime ... coincidence? Not for Charley Braggs. He left and took Melvina with him.

In the meantime Charley's mother supposedly died a natural death. As Charley was no longer around, Nannie was forced to work at the nearest cotton mill to support herself and Florine. He did eventually return, with another woman with another child. Charley was known as the 'husband who got away', but the future husbands were not so lucky.

Nannie then turned to the lonely-hearts column in the local paper, writing regularly to men whose advertisements were of interest to her. One response she received was from a 23-year-old factory worker by the name of Frank Harrelson. He wrote verse and sent an attractive photograph. Nannie was again besotted and sent him a cake, a picture of herself and encouraging words. He contacted her and they were subsequently married.

Unfortunately, Frank developed a strong liking for the drink and Nannie soon realised that her tall, handsome husband was becoming an alcoholic. As the years passed by, Nannie put up with Harrelson winding up in jail for drunk and disorderly behaviour, and doing the same at home. The marriage lasted 16 years.

By this time Nannie had refined her skills in murder, apparently on her two grandchildren: an infant girl and a two-year-old boy of her daughter, Melvina.

It was on the night of 15 September 1945 Frank Harrelson decided to go out to welcome home some friends from overseas, and get very drunk at the local tavern. Patriotism and the end of World War II were more than ample excuses.

Later that evening he arrived back home expecting an amorous night with Nannie. She wasn't interested.

Frank flew into a rage and as he hit the wall with his fist he shouted, 'If you don't listen to me, woman, I ain't gonna be here next week.'

These words, unfortunately, became quite prophetic, but not in the way Frank had intended. So, Nannie listened and complied with his wishes, to avoid another beating. But, she vowed to get even.

The opportunity arose the following day, as she was tending to her rose garden. There she found her husband's corn liquor jar hidden in the flower bed. She took the jar, emptied some of the contents, added some arsenical rat poison, and returned the jar to where she found it. That night Frank Harrelson died in agony from arsenic poisoning. He was only 38.

Nannie had now well and truly crossed the line.

And other lines she crossed as well including state ones, after her husband's death. It was the year of 1947, and Nannie found herself in Lexington, North Carolina in reply to another lonely-hearts advertisement.

Arlie Lanning was the next 'amour' as Nannie like to call her lovers. After meeting Nannie for the first time, they married two days later. But unfortunately for Nannie, Arlie was very much like her previous husband – he indulged in too much alcohol, and other females.

It now was starting to become a very familiar tale.

Nannie, not unexpectedly, took off without a word and stayed away for many weeks. Then suddenly, she reappeared and acted as the perfect domestic wife for the benefit of the Lexington onlookers. She also became a regular Methodist church goer and Arlie (when sober) would accompany his wife to Sunday morning services.

Arlie was supposedly the villain of the piece. So little sympathy unfortunately went to him when he subsequently died in February 1950. At the time it was considered to be heart failure. However, a number of things may have caused his heart to fail – including lying in pain for a couple of days before he died. As Nannie stated, 'He just sat down one morning to drink a cup of coffee and eat a bowl of prunes I especially prepared for him,' as folk gathered around for his funeral. 'Up until then, why let me tell you, he looked in fine shape. Then well, two days later, dead. I nursed him, and believe me, I nursed him, but I failed.' After dabbing her eyes with a handkerchief, she continued, 'Poor, poor Arlie. You know what he said to me before he breathed his last? He said, "Nannie, it must have been the coffee."'

Nannie proved to be quite the actress.

Following Arlie Lanning's death, Nannie decided to move in with his mother, Mrs Lanning senior, after the house they were living in burned to the ground on 21 April 1950. Nannie subsequently received an insurance cheque made out to her deceased husband, which she duly cashed as his widow. In the meantime, Mrs Lanning senior died in her sleep. It was time for Nannie to move on from North Carolina.

By 1952, at 47 years old, Nannie's figure had filled out, she now wore glasses and had a double chin. But while she had put on weight and she was starting to go grey, Nannie still had her girlish giggle to attract her next victim.

He was in the form of Richard Morton, a former salesman, who met Nannie through a dating club called The Diamond Circle Club. Richard was besotted by Nannie, so much so, he wrote to the club asking them to remove his and Nannie's names from the listings because she is '… the sweetest and most wonderful woman I have ever met.' They were married in October 1952 and she moved to his home in Emporia, Kansas.

For a time Nannie was happy in the arms of her new lover. However, within months of their marriage Richard Morton proved to be a disappointment to Nannie, and she was again answering advertisements from the various men in the Kansas newspapers. In the meantime, her father had died in Blue Mountain and her mother, Louisa decided to come and stay with the couple in the January 1953 – an unfortunate decision. After a couple of days with her daughter, she fell ill with severe stomach pains and died. It appears by all accounts that Nannie had carried out the most despicable act and murdered her own mother. Why she did this will never be known, but it is clear that Nannie now had no conscience or loyalty. Anyone who annoyed her or got in the way 'fell off the perch'.

Now it was Richard Morton's turn.

He followed soon after Louisa, three months later, and he too died after developing severe stomach pains.

Sam Doss had been one of Nannie's previous penpals, and after Richard Morton had passed away, she caught a bus to meet Sam in his hometown of Tulsa, Oklahoma. Sam Doss was quite unlike the other men that Nannie had met and subsequently married. Sam was solid, he was sturdy and a God-fearing man. He did not chase women, never drank, never smoked or gambled. At 59, his clean living belied his years, and his tidy manner and dress gave him a wealthy appearance. He proposed to Nannie in June 1953 and she accepted. They married and she was now Mrs Nannie Doss.

Unfortunately, Sam was set in his ways, and these irritated his less conservative wife. He had the view that 'Christian women don't need a television or romance magazines to be happy.' Nannie loved both – and she was no Christian!

The crunch came when he embarked on an austere lifestyle to save money. Nannie packed her bags and cleared off to Alabama. After she left, Sam sent her a number of letters pleading forgiveness. To show his sincerity, he gave her equal access to his bank finances and took out two life insurance policies naming her sole beneficiary.

The latter was a *very big* mistake.

Nannie did return, only to resume her evil ways. One September evening, after finishing dinner, Sam Doss also consumed some of Nannie's prune cake. That night Sam had severe stomach pains which continued for days. Eventually, his doctor sent him to hospital, where he stayed for just over three weeks. When he returned home, Nannie prepared a welcome home dinner which consisted of a pork roast washed down with coffee. That night Sam Doss passed away.

Dr Schwelbein, who had seen Sam prior to his release only the day before, was horrified to learn that his patient was dead. This did not make sense and he ordered an autopsy.

Nannie was just too impatient.

It was apparent from the autopsy report that Sam Doss did not die from natural causes or even from a severe digestive tract infection (which had been previously diagnosed). Instead, in his intestines and stomach were found the remains of a pork roast dinner and enough arsenic to kill a number of men!

Nannie was promptly arrested.

Initially, Nannie refused to accept her role in Sam Doss's death, which was hardly surprising. However, as the police insisted, arsenic does not come naturally in pork meat, nor in coffee. Certainly, not at the levels found in Sam Doss's body.

Sam had been admitted into hospital a month earlier, and he had consumed a plate of prune cake. The police then asked 'Was that poisoned too, Nannie?'

She replied, 'I don't know what you're talking about,' and giggled at their questioning saying, 'Me? Poison?'

She was interviewed for hours throughout which she continually flipped through the pages of her romance magazine. Amazingly, the police put up with this nonsense but they eventually said, 'Put the magazine down, Nannie, and listen to us. Nannie. Nannie? Look at us, why did you kill Doss?'

Further giggling, that 'sweet grandmother type', forever giggling.

'Nannie, we've been here for hours now, aren't you getting tired? You killed him, we know you killed him, you know you killed him.'

Nannie, 'Oh, boys, come on now, I killed nobody. I don't know why you think I did.'

Eventually, Police Agent Ray Page said, 'We've made phone calls, Nannie, and we've learned that Mr Doss was your fourth husband to die of the same symptoms. We're are putting two and two together, Nannie, and it looks like we just might come up with … well four. Arsenic, Nannie we believe they all died from arsenic. It will be easier if you admit what you have done, ahead of time. I mean, before we have to find out for ourselves …'

Nannie then said, 'Are you saying, young man, that I killed all of my husbands? You're a nice looking young man, but so foolish,' and then she returned to her magazine.

Agent Page's patience was finally exhausted and he said, 'No more reading, Nannie. This isn't a Christian Science reading room. You're gonna answer us,' and he took the magazine from her hands. He continued, 'Nannie, there are others too, aren't there? A lot of people around you dropped dead over the last couple of decades and their ghosts are coming back to haunt you. They're here, Nannie, in this room. Put 'em to rest, Nannie, put them to rest.'

It was time to stop messing around with Nannie Doss.

Police Agent Page knew there was more to her story. Nannie was evil, and he needed to remove the demon from her. Eventually, she said, 'All right, all right.' Then she began to talk.

Poisoning Sam Doss's coffee was because, 'He wouldn't let me watch my favourite programs on television, and he made me sleep without the fan on the hottest nights. He was a miser and well, what's a woman to do under those conditions?'

As you do.

When further pressed, with the offer to return her romance magazine, the confessions spilled out: Richard Morton, Arlie Lanning, Frank Harrelson and the death of Sam Doss. Each and every one of them a disappointment in the eyes of Nannie: 'If their ghosts are in this room they are either drunk or sleeping.'

Except for that solid man, Sam Doss.

With this information, the police detectives had their work cut out. There were victims in Kansas, North Carolina, Alabama and of course, the latest victim in Tulsa, Oklahoma. The bodies of her husbands, her mother, her sister Dovie, her nephew Robert and her mother-in-law, Arlie Lanning's mother, were exhumed. Their organs were tested, and found to contain lethal levels of arsenic. Surprise, surprise.

Bodies of other family members were also tested, but no arsenic was detected and it appeared they died from asphyxiation.

Nannie's first husband, Charley Braggs, asked that the bodies of his two daughters also be exhumed, along with the others. However, the Department of Justice indicated that they had enough on Nannie Doss to send her away for a very long time. A number of the deaths occurred in other states, namely Kansas, North Carolina and Alabama, and they wanted her for the deaths that occurred within their jurisdiction. But Nannie, unfortunately, was never tried outside Oklahoma.

Nannie Doss's trial was set for 2 June 1955 in the Criminal Court of Tulsa, Oklahoma. The prosecution's evidence was overwhelming. Nannie's murderous spree covering two decades was very damning.

On 17 May 1955 she decided to plead guilty. After a brief hearing, Judge Elmer Adams sentenced Nannie Doss to life imprisonment. She could have had the electric chair, but was spared because she was a woman. Nannie was then sent off to Oklahoma State Penitentiary for life.

In 1965, Nannie Doss died of cancer (leukaemia) in the prison's hospital ward. She was 60, and after some two decades of exposure to arsenic, the toxin she administered to her victims, she may well have also succumbed to its chronic effects. Arsenic is not only a toxin, but it can also cause various cancers at chronic low levels.

So, ironically, it is possible that nature finally carried out what the electric chair was denied.

But much closer to home. The next three stories involve a popular rat poison: 'Thall-rat' (readily available at the time in Sydney's rat-infested inner city) which contained the toxic, thallium sulphate.

These stories could easily be subtitled, 'Dark Dames and Dirty Rats'.

3.

DANCING WITH DEATH:
YVONNE FLETCHER

'Not forgiving is like drinking rat poison and waiting for the rat to die.'
– Anne Lamott

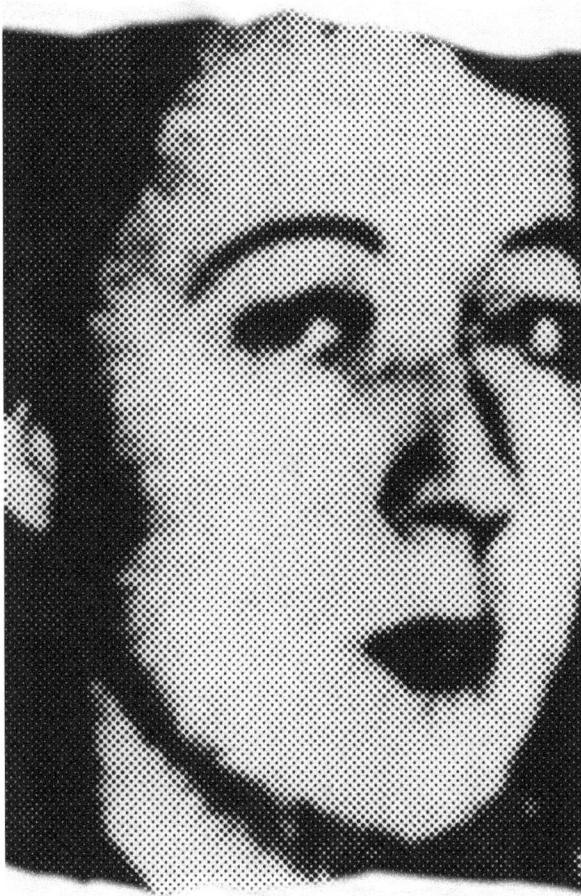

Ms Yvonne Gladys Fletcher.
PHOTOGRAPH COURTESY *of THE DAILY MIRROR*

The element thallium occurs in the mineral crookesite, a copper selenide, which contains 16 to 18 per cent thallium, and also contains 3 to 5 per cent silver. The mineral was named after the bright green colour it produced when its salts were put into a flame. William Crookes compared the colour to that of a fresh green shoot, and used the Greek word for this, which is *thallos*. Thallium salts have been used as baits to control rats, cockroaches, flies and ants. As the sulphate salt, the toxin was used in the infamous sticky fly papers that hung from the ceilings in many a suburban home in the fifties and sixties. Thallium is now mainly used in photoelectric cells and infrared detectors. The substance is now banned as a poison.

Thallium salts, such as the acetate and sulphate for example, are soluble in water and produce a colourless solution that is virtually tasteless. These properties would appear to make the poison a suitable homicidal agent. However, it has two major disadvantages. Firstly, the victim will recover from a less than fatal dose (unlike arsenic, which is cumulative), and obvious hair loss. In fact, thallium salts were once part of the medical pharmacopoeia and used to remove hair!

It was also used to remove a number of unfortunate people, as the following stories illustrate.

■

The reality of the 1950s in Australia was very different to the picture often shown today. Much of society was in upheaval following the return of soldiers from the war, often suffering from untreated war trauma and various injuries sustained in battle. Housing conditions were poor and often overcrowded – and there was a rat plague in inner Sydney. The government of the day decided to lift restrictions on the powerful rat poison thallium sulphate that killed both the rat that had eaten the bait and other rats that ate the subsequent corpse.

Unfortunately, thallium quickly became a popular drug used to poison people, as well as rats. A mineral discovered by Crookes now being *used by crooks* for their nefarious purposes! Being odourless and tasteless, it was easily added to food: it was cooked into cakes or scones and added to a drink or sweets. The first case came to court in 1952, sparking a recognition of thallium poisoning symptoms, and more cases came to light.

Yvonne Fletcher hailed from Newtown, an inner-city suburb of Sydney, and loved fashion and dancing. Her true passions. It was through the latter that she met both of her husbands. Her favourite dances were the jitterbug and the foxtrot, both popular dances at the time.

However, her most desired 'dance partner' was freedom. She had no time for the clearly defined gender roles and expectations of men, women and families in the 1950s. Women were not expected to have a career and became dependent on men for financial support and status. The restrictions on women in mainstream Australian culture at that time didn't rest easy with Yvonne Fletcher. She sought release by using a subtle, readily available poison which would lead the men in her life to their deaths, the poison to achieve her nefarious outcome in this final dance of death was thallium.

The silent killer.

Newtown originally was established as a residential and farming area in the early 19th century. The town took its name from a grocery store opened there by John and Margaret Webster in 1832, at a site close to where the Newtown railway station stands today. They placed a sign over their store that said 'New Town Stores'. Eventually, the name New Town was adopted, at first unofficially, with the space disappearing to form the name Newtown.

The streets of Newtown, Sydney back in the 1940s and 1950s were very different from today. The inner-city suburb had a chronic rat problem, with an estimated population of up to *two million* rats in inner Sydney by the late 1940s. Rats are known carriers of disease, such as the well-known bubonic plague (or Black Death), a variety of bacterial infections including diphtheria and salmonellosis, a number of haemorrhagic fevers and tularaemia (also called 'rabbit fever', a rare infectious disease that typically attacks the skin, eyes, lymph nodes and lungs). Rats were also a menace in family homes, having been found nibbling on the faces, hair and feet of small children leading to rat-bite fever (sometimes called Haverhill fever or epidemic arthritic erythema).

Another job for the ever popular rat killer, Thall-Rat?

Clearly, Yvonne Fletcher thought so. The young mother was caught up in an unhappy marriage to Desmond George Butler. But worse, he wound up spending two years in jail. During this difficult time, Yvonne cared for their children and saved what money she could, only for it to be squandered on frivolous things when he was finally released from jail.

Given the years Desmond was in jail, and then released to further complicate her life, along with occasional violence, led to a 'black hatred' of her husband. He had been treated by Dr K. King at Callan Park Hospital for the Insane (it is located in an area on the shores of Iron Cove in Lilyfield, a suburb of Sydney. Yvonne told the doctor she could not cope with her husband and his behaviour and asked whether he could be readmitted.

Unfortunately for all parties, this did not eventuate at the making.

The thought of using Thall-Rat to bring some peace into her life had no doubt become irresistible. When Dr King again visited Desmond Butler on 27 July 1948 on a follow-up call, he found the formerly fit, strong, albeit neurotic man, was now a 'helpless, protoplasmic mess – like a jelly'. He was now incapable of moving and throwing objects, which had included food(!) As such Dr King arranged for Butler to be admitted to Broughton Hall for treatment the following day at 11 am.

Desmond George Butler passed away shortly after on 29 July 1948. Yvonne wasn't at home when police called around to her home to break the news of her husband's death. However, the following day she fainted when told the news and was surprised that she had to attend the hospital to identify her husband's body, thinking it might have been her brother involved in a motorcycle accident.

After formal identification, Desmond Butler's body was conveyed to the morgue on 31 July 1948 where Dr Sheldon performed a post-mortem. In view of negative tests for arsenic and lead at Prince Alfred Hospital, he did not send the organ samples on for further analysis, especially for thallium.

A subsequent inquest on 20 August 1948 presided over by City Coroner, Mr Austin found that Desmond Butler died from 'natural causes pertaining to peripheral neuritis of unknown origin affecting the heart.'

It appeared Yvonne had got away with allegedly murdering her annoying first husband! After a couple of years had passed, the very social Yvonne was lonely with only her children for company, and sorely needed adult male company. This came in the form of a fellow dancer, Bertram Henry Fletcher. Their eyes met across the dance hall and they became besotted lovers.

On 17 November 1951 Bertram Henry Fletcher married Yvonne Gladys Butler. Unfortunately, the sweet domestic bliss was short lived.

Mrs Yvonne Gladys Fletcher and Mr Bertram ('Bluey') Henry Fletcher in happier days. PHOTOGRAPH COURTESY OF *TRUTH* (SYDNEY) 28 SEPTEMBER 1952

The now Mrs Fletcher was realising that her handsome husband, who was employed as a foreman at Butler & Norman's, Alexandria, laying rat baits was also a rat! And a violent one at that.

By January and February of 1952 Yvonne Fletcher had applied to the court for protection from assaults and sought an apprehended violence order (AVO) against Bertram (appropriately nicknamed, 'Bluey') Fletcher.

On 8 March 1952 Bertram Fletcher left Butler & Norman's feeling quite sick. The day previously, he had had a 'terrible row' with his wife. No doubt over the AVO. He called into the home of his sister, Mrs Florence Witchard, at 11am complaining to her that, 'My feet feel funny – pins and needles.'

Clearly, a thallium poisoning was afoot (excuse the pun).

The following day a next-door neighbour, Roy Stewart, heard Bertram Fletcher moving about in his backyard at about 5.30 pm, clearly in distress. He went to his aid after being called. Fletcher said to his neighbour, 'My feet are all numb and I can't walk.'

Mr Stewart kindly called the ambulance, which took Fletcher to the Royal Prince Alfred Hospital in nearby Camperdown for treatment. A clearly distressed Bluey Fletcher was examined by medical staff and tried to contact his wife, without success. Instead they contacted Mrs Witchard, who came to the hospital at 2 am and took him back to her home where she nursed him. When visited by his father, Bluey mentioned to him that his hands were numb. This complaint resulted in a follow-up examination by Dr Thomson, who after examining Fletcher, declared that his symptoms were 'consistent with peripheral neuritis'. (The same diagnosis given for Desmond Butler's symptoms.)

Then on 12 March 1952 Dr Thomson again visited Bluey Fletcher, given his sister's grave concerns. She had been combing his hair and it was now falling out in clumps.

Dr Thomson arranged another admission to Royal Prince Alfred Hospital and mentioned to the hospital medical superintendent the suspicion of a poisoning. However, the usual tests for arsenic and lead, not surprisingly, were negative. Unfortunately, the poison, thallium hadn't been considered in the testing regimen.

In the meantime, Mrs Yvonne Fletcher attended a meeting with Mr Hawkins, a public solicitor, and said to him, 'It all came back to me about Bluey [Fletcher] saying he would take poison and get me into trouble.' It appeared Yvonne was covering her back.

Sadly, on 23 March 1952 Bertram Henry Fletcher died. The following day his body was taken to the Glebe Department of Forensic Medicine where he was identified by Mrs Yvonne Fletcher and by doctors Sheldon and Percy. The organ samples were sent to the government analyst for analysis prior to police investigations. Curiously, again the organ and blood samples were *not* screened for the presence of thallium. It was only after the similarities in the deaths that suspicions were aroused to such an extent that Mrs Fletcher complained to Dr Thomson that she was upset by the rumours that she had poisoned her second husband – not to mention her first husband!

Nevertheless, on 17 April 1952, the city coroner, Mr F. J. Forrest, based on the evidence in a brief before him, issued an order for the exhumation of Desmond Butler's body. This decision would not have been undertaken lightly, as exhumations are rare and are often traumatic for the family members involved.

On 22 April 1952 Dr Percy and Dr Sheldon performed further post-mortems on the remains with appropriate samples being sent to the government analyst for examination.

Just over a fortnight later, on 10 May 1952 the government analyst reported that the remains contained a 'heavy infusion of thallium'. The examining doctors were now of the opinion that the deceased had died from thallium poisoning.

The findings were reported to the homicide squad who on 19 May 1952 had Mrs Fletcher arrested and charged with murdering both her husbands. As police took Mrs Fletcher away, her neighbour, seeing the proceedings, waved to her, to which she responded by laughing and saying, 'I'm being arrested.'

A curious response.

Several inquests were requested before the matter finally went to court. Eventually, the matter wound up at Sydney Central Criminal Court on 22 September 1952, where Mrs Yvonne Fletcher was brought to trial for the murders of Desmond Butler and Bertram Fletcher.

Mr Justice Kinsella was presiding and ruled that the Crown could lead evidence of Bertram Fletcher's death. He continued that this would not be admitted to prove Butler had been poisoned by Mrs Fletcher, but only to exclude the possibility that Butler had been poisoned accidentally, had committed suicide, or, maybe, had been poisoned by someone unknown.

Mrs Yvonne Fletcher sat patiently in the dock while the Crown Prosecutor, Mr Rooney, QC led the evidence into the deaths of her husbands. The Crown alleged that the deaths of her first husband, Desmond Butler was through thallium poisoning. Two doctors were called to give expert evidence that her second husband, Bertram Henry Fletcher, whom she married in November of the previous year, had also died from thallium poisoning.

Sydney Central Criminal Court, Liverpool Street, Sydney.

Mrs Fletcher steadfastly maintained her innocence stating, 'I never poisoned my husbands.'

She continued in a low but clear voice, 'I do not know who poisoned them or how they were poisoned. I have never bought or handled any poisons at any time.' Then turning to the jury she continued in the same low voice, 'And you know as much about the deaths of these two men as I do. The only poison I know anything about is that Mr Fletcher brought home some rat poison, and he was sitting and pouring some stuff like water on to a saucer, and on to bread, and put them under the house, and that was all I saw of these.' Further reiterating her innocence she said, 'I got nothing out of their deaths. I had to borrow £10 on my first husband's funeral expenses, and I paid the rest off at the rate of £1 a week. I have not yet paid for my second husband's funeral. I had both my children insured, but had no insurance on my husbands.'

The latter appeared to exclude motive.

Mrs Fletcher continued her statement saying, 'When Des came home from hospital he was still very sick. He was very bad the first night, and the very next day I was on Dr King's doorstep. Des was only home for a week, and I had to be in and out all the time. I had to buy food and look after my children. I had to see Dr King and Dr Kirkwood, and I had to buy food and look after my children.'

She further added, 'I had to go down and see about an invalid pension for him [Desmond Butler], the forms were filled in, but he died before they were posted.'

She was further questioned about the care she administered and the social services sought. Mrs Fletcher replied by saying that, 'It is cruel lies to say that I was not there all the time, I told them [it was] the best I could after five years gone by.'

When questioned about her marriage and relationship with Bertram 'Bluey' Fletcher she replied, 'After I married Fletcher I was very happy for a while. His manner changed suddenly. He started to accuse me of poisoning my first husband, but I do not why he said that. I think somebody must have told him those things. He was a moody man. He would not answer while he said those things. He was very evasive. I told him I was taking steps to have him ejected from the house and it was then he said he would take poison to get me into trouble.'

At this point Mrs Fletcher paused and was offered a glass of water and rested for a while. It had been a very long day.

Then Mr Reginald W. Hawkins, public solicitor for New South Wales, arose from his seat and addressed the court saying that in February that year Mrs Fletcher had applied for legal assistance for the removal of Bertram Fletcher from their premises in Ferndale Street, Newtown. However, because of certain proceedings in the Newtown Court the application wasn't processed. An unfortunate turn of events, which may have saved Bertram Fletcher's life.

The public defender, Mr. F. Vizzard, then asked if Mrs Fletcher mentioned anything about the poisoning on the second occasion.

Mr Hawkins replied that she had said he (Fletcher) had threatened to take poison to make himself sick to get her in trouble if she continued with these proceedings. A curious defence. But I did have an arsenic poisoning case ('Arsenic for Dinner?') some three decades later where a husband did indeed take low doses of arsenic to implicate his wife in attempted murder – and it almost succeeded!

The Crown then brought forth the father of the deceased, Henry Fletcher, to provide evidence. It must have been a tough call for the man, who said that soon after their marriage he had counselled his son and his daughter-in-law about their matrimonial unhappiness and unsuccessfully tried to mediate between them.

Another witness, Mrs Edith Roach of Ferndale Street, Newtown, described how she had seen Mrs Fletcher with sticking plaster on her head. When asked what happened, she said her husband had hit her on her head with a key.

Mrs Roach then described another occasion where she saw Mrs Fletcher holding a bloodstained handkerchief to her face saying, 'What do you think of that fellow of mine? He is trying to tell everyone that he is going like Dessie, and if he keeps that up I will be put in gaol.' She then told Mrs Fletcher not to get upset because if 'she had done nothing at all the police in Sydney cannot touch you'.

Further questions were asked to Sydney George Woods, a foreman at Butler & Norman, where Bertram Fletcher had been employed, supposedly as a bottler sorter. He said that about a fortnight earlier, before he became sick, Fletcher had asked him for some poison to use as rat bait. He then said he gave him a bottle of Thall-Rat.

Detective Sergeant Donald Fergusson then took the stand and was questioned about his interview of Mrs Fletcher. He said that on 19 May 1952 he interviewed Mrs Fletcher at the District Criminal Investigation

Branch (CIB) and informed her that thallium had been detected in Bertram Fletcher's body. She appeared surprised and asked, 'How did he get that?' and added, that she had no knowledge of thallium and asked what it was used for. The detective replied that thallium was used to poison rats.

Detective Fergusson continued his evidence that Mrs Fletcher told him that her husband had brought home some rat poison about six weeks earlier and had used it all on baited bread. She clearly knew that the poison was used for the eradication of rats.

During the police interview Mrs Fletcher described her husband as a very moody man, and said they often had quarrels, and that he had given 'her a terrible time'. She also mentioned how her husband hit her little boy 'making him black and blue'.

Detective Fergusson said during the interview that Mrs Fletcher considered divorcing her husband due to the violence he meted out to his family.

With this, the court was subsequently adjourned.

On 23 September 1952 Mrs Yvonne Fletcher was found guilty by the Central Criminal Court jury after a four-hour deliberation, on the charge of having murdered her first husband, Desmond George Butler, 'by administering thallium'. She showed no emotion when the foreman of the jury announced the verdict.

Mrs Fletcher was then asked whether she had anything to say before passing sentence and replied, 'No, your Honour.'

Mr Justice Kinsella then said in a clear voice, 'You have had a fair trial and a patient and careful consideration of the evidence by the jury. If the conviction had been in respect of your second husband, possibly some palliation of your crime might be found, the evidence showed you suffered greatly at his hands. In respect to your first husband, there is no evidence at all of that nature. The crime of murder is a terrible one and when the killing is by means of an insidious poison, secretly administered within the family circle to an unsuspecting victim, which destroyed him mentally and physically, while permitting him to linger for months in wretched agony, then the crime is a horrible one.'

During the judge's address, Mrs Fletcher constantly opened and closed her eyes. When he concluded with passing the death sentence saying, 'For the crime of murder, the law of this State, has one sentence, death.' Adding, 'I, therefore, sentence you, Yvonne Gladys Fletcher to death.'

She suddenly went white, swayed and then collapsed in the dock, dropping her prayer book, which she had brought with her during the seven-day trial. Whether this was for dramatic effect or genuine remorse, we'll never know. Nevertheless, three policewomen and a male constable rushed to her aid and provided her with a glass of water. As two policewomen led her down to the cells, she suddenly burst into a flood of tears. Most likely, realising the enormity of the offence she committed.

Mrs Fletcher subsequently, appealed against the conviction. However, the State Full Court dismissed the appeal in February 1953, the following year. She had also been charged with the murder of her second husband, Bertram Fletcher 'by the administration of thallium' but the Crown surprisingly decided not to proceed with this latter charge.

Mrs Fletcher was placed in an observation cell at Long Bay until her sentence was carried out or commuted to a term of imprisonment. A jail authority said that if the sentence was commuted to imprisonment for life, Mrs Fletcher would be able to petition for release after 20 years while she remained at Long Bay. Fortunately for her, the death sentence would be commuted a few years later when the New South Wales government abolished the death penalty for murder in 1955.

Yvonne Fletcher would eventually leave prison as a free woman in 1964 after serving a good deal less than 20 years for the murders, to then slip into anonymity.

During Yvonne Fletcher's trial, Mr Justice Kinsella made a recommendation the jury that, in view of the scientific evidence, the sale of thallium poison in any form to the general public should be prohibited. He said he would pass this recommendation onto the appropriate authority.

Unfortunately, this was too little, too late for the next cases …

4.

PASTRIES AND POISON: CAROLINE GRILLS

'Let's just say you may regret that second piece of cake.
Oh my God, regret cake?
Whatever was about to happen must be truly evil.'
— Rachel Hawkins, *Hex Hall*

A smiling Caroline Grills looked like a decent person.
PHOTOGRAPH COURTESY OF *THE DAILY TELEGRAPH*

Another infamous thallium poisoner of the time was Caroline Grills, or 'Aunt Carrie', as she was known. She appeared to be a most unlikely multiple murderer, being a friendly 63-year-old mother, grandmother and great-grandmother – another smiling murderer (see earlier Nannie Doss).

She was charged with having murdered four members of her family and attempted to murder another three by adding thallium to her homemade treats including fresh scones and cakes.

A face like a 'fresh warm scone – buttered in evil'.

■

Caroline Grills's first victim was her stepmother, Mrs Christina Mickelson, who died suddenly. This was not too surprising as she was, after all, 87 years old. Nor did it seem strange that a family friend, another old lady in her eighties, died soon after. However, another relative, John Lunberg, who was only 60, fell ill after visiting Aunt Carrie. He lost all of his hair and died in 1948. He was soon followed by Mary Anne Mickelson.

Caroline Grills was still busy.

Her next victim was Lundberg's widow Eveline, and her daughter also began to lose her hair and feeling from her limbs. Clearly deliberate poisoning was afoot.

A suspicious son-in-law of one of her intended victims, already suffering the effects as a result of a previous poisoning, one day noticed Caroline Grills carrying a cup of tea. She placed her hand into her dress pocket and then put it over the cup as if dropping something into the tea. The son-in-law switched the cup, surreptitiously poured the tea into a bottle and gave it to police, who forwarded the specimen on to a toxicology laboratory.

Smart move. It was found to contain a lethal dose of thallium. Mrs Grills was promptly arrested.

The bodies of two of her previous victims were then exhumed and found to contain traces of thallium. Two others thought to have been poisoned had been cremated. Police found traces of thallium in the pocket of the dress Mrs Grills had worn on the day she tried to give the cup of tea to the last victim. The day of reckoning was rapidly approaching.

At the Supreme Court in Sydney, Mr Tedeschi, Crown Prosecutor, said in his opening address, 'Seven people were the recipients of charity and kindness from Aunt Carrie [as she was known].' He then continued, 'They had died or suffered the horrible effects of thallium poisoning. Sometimes she had a financial benefit to gain, and sometimes none'.

Mrs Grills proved to be as eccentric as she was deadly, and her defence council had to caution her on a number of occasions not to chuckle or make comments in court while evidence was being presented.

Senior Crown Prosecutor Mick Rooney QC alleged that she was '… a killer who poisoned … for sport, for fun, for the kicks she got out of it, for the hell of it, for the thrill that she and she alone in the world knew the cause of the victims' suffering.'

The jury took only 12 minutes to find her guilty of murder – and the death sentence. Mrs Grills was then led out of the dock, amazingly, smiling and singing, 'We're off to see the wizard …' She was truly weird, a total fruit loop – and very dangerous!

A subsequent 1950s newspaper headline read:

MRS GRILLS DENIED LEAVE OF APPEAL

The Court of Criminal Appeal in a reserved judgment yesterday refused Mrs. Caroline Grills leave to appeal against her conviction for the attempted murder of her sister-in-law, Mrs. Eveline Lundberg, by thallium poisoning.

Mrs. Grills, 63, of Gerrish Street, Gladesville, is the wife of a city estate agent.

She was convicted at the Central Criminal Court last year on a charge of having administered thallium to Mrs. Lundberg, 67, at Redfern, on April 20, 1953, with intent to murder her. She was sentenced to death.

However, her death sentence was later commuted to life.

This jovial, and very eccentric 63-year-old serial killer was to spend the rest of her days in Long Bay Gaol, where she became known by the other inmates as 'Aunt Thally'.

She eventually died in 1960, after she was taken to Prince Henry Hospital suffering from peritonitis, eventually succumbing to complications from a ruptured gastric ulcer. Yes, she eventually got life.

Sometimes justice does prevail.

5.

RATS AND RUGBY:
THE VERONICA MONTY CASE

'Sinful and forbidden pleasures are like poisoned bread;
They may satisfy appetite for the moment, but there is
death in them at the end.'
— Tryon Edwards

Veronica Monty: a very affectionate mother-in-law.
PHOTOGRAPH COURTESY OF *THE COURIER-MAIL*

Over many decades, sport has had its controversies, not the least of which have involved rugby league in Australia. These have included drug usage, alleged rape, money issues, fake medical situations and sex scandals. To name but a few.

But this story includes it all: adultery, a celebrity, attempted murder, an attempted suicide, divorce and the end of a talented sportsman's career. But what kicked-off this awful football tale? It involved a very promising footballer, his beautiful wife and a very randy mother-in-law.

A salacious love triangle was about to develop.

■

Robert ('Bobby') Lulham was born in Newcastle on 2 November 1926 and began playing in the New South Wales rugby league competition in his mid-teens. He subsequently moved to Sydney to play for the Balmain Tigers in 1947. It wasn't long before it became apparent that Lulham was a talented player, particularly in the winger position. In his debut season for Balmain, he became the season's top try scorer with an amazing 28 tries, a Balmain club record that still stands to this day. He was selected to play for New South Wales in all four games, as well as playing for Balmain in their 13–7 grand final win over Canterbury. Heady days!

This was followed up a year later when Lulham made his debut for Australia in the third test against Great Britain. He scored a try in this Test, but unfortunately Australia lost 23–9. He played two more Tests on the Kangaroo tour against France in 1948–49.

It looked a very promising future for the young footballer with the possibility of Bobby Lulham becoming a footy superstar. Until the 1953 NRL footy season.

It was soon noticed that Lulham's performance was well below his usually high standard of play. He fobbed it off saying that he had an off day. Given his reputation, the officials accepted the explanation and did not pursue the matter further.

But sadly, much more was afoot.

Two years earlier, in 1951, Mrs Veronica Mabel Monty had separated from her husband, Alfred, and appeared to have nowhere to live during this difficult period. Her daughter, Judith Lulham, kindly offered her a place to stay until things were settled. It turned out to be a most unfortunate arrangement. Bobby and Veronica, his mother-in-law, soon started a sexual relationship.

Even so, Lulham still played talented football, despite the stresses of adultery and running his own small business as a truck driver.

Things came to a head after a game against the St George Dragons at Leichhardt Oval on 11 July 1953, where he successfully scored a try and kicked seven goals. However, the following week on the same ground it was quite a different story. He became very ill before the game against the Canterbury-Bankstown Bulldogs, complaining of pain in his feet and numbness in his legs. The next day his hair started to fall out in clumps and he was rushed to hospital. There tests revealed that he had ingested over half the lethal dose of the rat poison, thallium.

Police were promptly notified, and two weeks after the discovery, Lulham's mother-in-law was arrested and charged with administering thallium to Lulham with intent to murder him. Veronica Monty had commented earlier that she didn't know why anyone would want to poison Bobby as he was considered, 'one of the most popular boys in the district'.

But, as in most cases, the truth emerges eventually.

Veronica Monty admitted she was feeling very guilty about deceiving her daughter, and was feeling depressed about the situation. So she decided to talk to Bobby about their relationship before it wrecked her daughter's marriage. She had prepared two cups of Milo for Bobby and herself and had put the rat poison in one of the cups. She had intended to tell him she couldn't live with the guilt anymore and decided to kill herself.

Unfortunately, it appeared the drinks became mixed up and Bobby drank the poisoned beverage – with the dire results that occurred before the Canterbury-Bankstown match.

Possibly realising the enormity of what she had done, Veronica Monty tried to cover her tracks and made an anonymous phone call to police, saying her estranged husband had put the rat poison in Bobby's beer. It was a bit of a tall tale, as Bobby had little to do with estranged Alfred Monty and vice versa due to work commitments. Eventually, Mrs Monty admitted that as tensions grew in the Lulham home, she decided to end the affair, with the subsequent outcome.

The matter went to Central Police Court on 9 September 1953, where Mrs Veronica Mabel Monty was brought to trial for the attempted murder of star footballer Robert ('Bobby') John Lulham. The case had become a media circus with headlines now emblazoned:

'My mother was my husband's lover.'
'Pretty wife's allegations in Bobby Lulham poisoning case.'

Mrs Judy Lulham, 21, said that he mother, charged with having given Lulham thallium, had admitted to intimacy with him three times. She told the court she had discovered Bobby and her mother had sex on a Sunday morning while she was at mass, again while listening to the Test cricket on the radio while she was asleep in the house, and on another occasion when Bobby took a 'sickie' from work.

When Mrs Monty was asked what led up to her behaviour, she replied, 'It just sort of happened on the lounge. A kiss, and well, one thing led to another …'

Police witnesses were called before the court and spoke of admissions during their interviews, where Mrs Monty admitted to intercourse between her and Bobby Lulham. Further admissions were made concerning a strange telephone call to the CIB in which a sobbing woman's voice said someone had put thallium in a drink at the Lulham home.

A statement provided by Mrs Monty said that she had put thallium in a drink for herself, but must have given it instead to Bobby Lulham while he was in bed with his wife.

Further evidence was provided by Detective Sergeant George Davis, that he and Detective Constable Paul followed up on this information and visited the Lulham home in Hinkler Avenue, Ryde on 20 July, after a telephone call from Dr Greenberg of Macquarie Street. He was said to have received a message from a woman who claimed that her husband had put rat poison in Bobby Lulham's beer.

Detective Davis went on to say that when he interviewed Mrs Monty on 6 August at the CIB, she said she believed 'her daughter's marriage had not turned out as well as expected'. When further questioned about this, she replied, 'Bobby has been getting home later from training. One morning I found lipstick and make-up on his shirt, and every football match we go to Gwen Stuart is there.'

He continued on, saying that Mrs Monty admitted to the fact that she and Bobby had been intimate one night when they were listening to the cricket on the radio, and again when he came home from work supposedly sick. Further she admitted to making the phone calls to the CIB and to Dr Greenberg.

Detective Davis said that Mrs Monty also told him, 'One night I was down in the dumps. I was going to have a hot drink, and I put some thallium in it. When I went to pick up the cups I must have picked up the wrong one. I took the hot drinks to Bobby and Judy, but I really thought I was the one who was getting the poison.'

Mrs Judy Lulham later gave evidence on 27 July and said that after her husband had gone to hospital, her mother told her that she and Bobby had become intimate. She added that on one occasion they had sex while Mrs Lulham was at mass. It was a tangled love triangle that wasn't to have a happy finale.

Nevertheless, the jury found Mrs Monty not guilty of attempted murder, and the case ended with mother and daughter, ironically, both former lovers of the Australian rugby league star, Bobby Lulham, tearfully embracing each other in court.

But, as they say, it's not truly over until the paperwork in done.

The following year, Judy Lulham filed for divorce, citing her mother as co-respondent. Mr Alfred Monty then sued his wife for divorce, citing his son-in-law, Bobby Lulham, as co-respondent.

The following newspaper headlines said it all:

'Two divorce suits filed' *Sydney Morning Herald*, 3 October 1955

Double divorce suits have been filed in the Bobby Lulham poisoning case have been filed.

Mrs Judy Lulham is filing for divorce of her husband, Bobby Lulham, Rugby

League football star, naming her mother, Mrs. Veronica Monty, as co-respondent.

Mr Alfred Monty named Lulham, his son-in-law, as co-respondent in his suit for divorce.

Mrs Monty was acquitted by Central Criminal Court jury on December 10 last year of having attempted to poison Lulham with thallium.

The Crown alleged at the trial that Mrs Monty had attempted to poison Lulham to prevent her daughter of learning of her intimacies with him.

The Crown alleged that when questioned by police Mrs Monty admitted to mixing the poison, but claimed she meant it for herself.

Interviewed at his home at Ryde yesterday, Lulham admitted her had not been served the divorce papers.

He said her had not seen his wife or Mrs Monty since the trial. He had been staying with his parents at Tuncurry and only returned to Sydney a few weeks ago.

Sadly, after these suits were filed and finalised, Mrs Veronica Monty took her life by shooting herself in 1955 at a North Sydney hotel.

Bobby Lulham never played rugby league again and retired to Tenterfield, where he died of a heart attack in 1986 aged 60.

It was reported that about 46 cases of thallium poisonings occurred in Sydney between March 1952 and May 1953, 10 of which resulted in fatalities. However, by the end of 1953, six women in New South Wales had been charged with poisoning family members with thallium.

Of the six accused thallium poisoners, the trials of Yvonne Fletcher, Veronica Monty and Caroline Grill provoked massive media frenzies.

Fortunately for the people of New South Wales, the sensational coverage of the Lulham poisoning forced the hand of the New South Wales Government to place restrictions on the sale of Thall-Rat. And hopefully, the lessons learnt from the two earlier sensational cases prevented further loss of life from this awful insidious poison.

But what made these poisonings unusual is that they were carried out by women within the seemingly safe setting of the home. Their offerings of food and drink were really murder attempts cleverly disguised as acts of generosity. Chillingly, none of these women offered worthwhile reasons for why they were so set on murdering, or at the very least severely incapacitating, their family members.

But next cases are quite different and possibly more repellent, where a mother murders her own children.

6.

MUM THE MURDERER: DIANE DOWNS

*'I stare at Diane's smile. I would die for that,
though I barely understand why.'*
– Frank J. Fleming, *Supergo: Fathom*

Elizabeth Diane Frederickson-Downs. (c. 1984)

Diane Downs was born in Phoenix, Arizona on 7 August 1955 as Elizabeth Diane Frederickson Downs to parents, Wesley Linden and Willadene (Engle) Frederickson. She subsequently moved to Springfield, Oregon, where this story unfolds.

Springfield was named after a natural spring found in a field within the current city boundaries. The city is located in the southern Willamette Valley, on the Pacific north-west of the United States. The Willamette River flows along the whole length of the Willamette Valley, a 250-kilometre-long valley (150 miles) flanked by mountains on three sides namely, the Oregon Coast Range to the west, the Cascade Coast Range to the east, and the Calapooya Mountains to south. The valley is said to be synonymous with the 'cultural and political heart of Oregon'.

The city's economy was initially mainly based on the Oregon timber industry, however, since the 1990s the economy has diversified. It was in this setting that this infamous case of filicide (child murder) occurred.

■

It was a quiet night on a warm evening of 19 May 1983 in Springfield, Oregon in the north-west of the United States when a telephone call came into the Springfield Police Department (SPD) at 10.40 pm: 'Employee of McKenzie-Willamette Hospital advises of gunshot victims at that location. Officers dispatched. Arrived 10.48 pm.'

The McKenzie-Willamette Hospital emergency room at that time was a rather humble facility, which was somewhat cramped, with painted walls and baseboards that had been scrubbed dull and drab and the waiting room comprised of chrome furniture with aged vinyl. The emergency room that evening shift was staffed by a night receptionist, Judy Patterson, Rosie Martin, a registered nurse (RN) and Shelby Day, a licensed practical nurse (LPN). The physician-in-charge that evening was Dr John Mackey. (RNs provide nursing care which includes primary administration of medication and treatments along with medical advice to patients. LPNs provide more basic nursing care and ensure the comfort of patients.)

A persistent car horn drew the attention of the medical staff. The two nurses hurried out to the emergency drive-through. Rosie Martin, seeing the car parked there asked the blonde-haired driver, 'What's going on here?'

'Somebody just shot my kids!' came the awful reply.

Examination of the blood-splattered vehicle by the medical staff revealed the presence of three severely injured children from gunshot wounds and the driver, who gave her name as Diane Downs, with a gunshot wound to her left forearm.

It was a tragic scene. The eldest child, Christie Ann (eight years) had suffered a disabling stroke from her injuries, Cheryl Lyn (seven) was dead and Stephen 'Danny' (three) Downs was paralysed from the waist down where the bullet had slammed into his back close to the T6 and T7 vertebrae of his spine. But for the skilled surgery carried out, it may well have been a triple tragedy.

However, the medical staff were astonished at Diane Downs's calm demeanour during the terrible ordeal and put it down to a strong woman able to hold her emotions in. She explained to the receptionist that she was carjacked on a rural road, Old Mohawk Road near Springfield, by a strange, bushy-haired man who shot her three children and her in the arm when he tried to wrestle the car keys from her. Downs said she got into the car and rushed her injured children to hospital. She insisted that the man was still out there and so the receptionist duly called the Springfield Police Department.

Police investigators swung into action, as the story became headlines in local and state newspapers based on Diane Downs's assertion that there was a mad gunman on the loose.

It was a worrying time for the town's citizens, as the story initially appeared credible and a manhunt was underway. However, as the search went on with neither weapon nor suspect found, detectives were beginning to suspect Downs. They noticed discrepancies in Diane Downs's version of the events that occurred on the fateful evening throughout their police interviews with her. And forensic evidence did not support her statements; there was no blood splatter on the driver's side of the car, nor was there gunpowder residue on the driver's door or on the interior door panel given the close encounter by the assailant.

Detectives then searched Diane Downs's apartment seeking evidence that may shed light on the case. Their findings were quite surprising.

A series of love letters to a married man and co-worker in Arizona with whom she had been having an extramarital affair, along with a diary where her main love interest made it plain he didn't want children. This in itself, this was not strong evidence – but it certainly suggested motive.

There seem to be some discrepancies over who Diane Downs's love interest was which apparently lead to the tragic outcomes. Was it Robert Knickerbocker and/or Lew Lewiston as suggested in Ann Rule's novel Small Sacrifices? Nevertheless it appears a married man was involved and Diane was said to be besotted by him after she had separated (later divorced) from her estranged husband, Steve Downs.

Diane Downs did not reveal to police that she had in her possession a .22 calibre handgun, the same type that was used to shoot the children. However, both Steve Downs and her alleged lover told police that she did. Further investigations revealed that the handgun was purchased in Arizona. While the actual weapon was not found, they did find unfired bullet casings in her home with extractor markings from the murder weapon. Based on this and other evidence gathered, Diane Downs was arrested on 28 February 1984, some nine months after the shooting, and charged with one count of murder, two counts each of attempted murder and criminal assault.

Curiously, prior to her arrest Ms Downs became pregnant with a fifth child and gave birth to a girl, whom she named Amy Elizabeth, just a month after her 1984 trial. Then ten days before her sentencing, the baby girl Amy was taken into the care of the state of Oregon and was subsequently adopted by Chris and Jackie Babcock, who renamed her, Rebecca.

It appeared at the outset that Diane's motive was simple: she just wanted to get rid of the kids, so the path was clear for her to be with her lover. As the matter subsequently went before the courts, prosecutors argued that Diane Downs shot her children to be free of them so she could continue her affair with her lover.

The most damning testimony came from several sources, including her surviving daughter, Christie, who once she recovered from her awful injuries which included a stroke, and was eventually able to speak, said how her mother shot her and her two siblings while parked on the side of the road and then shot herself in the arm. When questioned if she remembered the strange shaggy haired man who allegedly shot her and her brother and sister, she said no. Nurses who gave evidence said that her vitals while in intensive care, would spike when her mother Diane Downs, entered the ward room. Was she scared or happy to see her mum?

Diane Downs had been diagnosed with narcissistic, antisocial and histrionic (dramatic or theatrical traits – essentially attention seeking) personality disorders.

On 17 June 1984, Diane Downs was convicted on all charges and sentenced to life in prison plus 50 years. Even so she was required to serve 25 years before being considered for parole. Essentially she was *never to be released*. It was clear that the judge did not intend for Ms Downs to ever be free again.

The lead prosecutor on the case, Mr Fred Hugi and his wife Joanne subsequently adopted the two surviving children in 1986.

Diane Downs was incarcerated at the Oregon Women's Correctional Centre in Salem, and there the matter appeared to have ended with Downs serving out her sentence. But it wasn't to be so.

Three years after being sentenced, on 11 July 1987, Diane Downs escaped from prison. She was caught just a few blocks away from the prison on 21 July. For the escape from custody, she received a further five years added to her already hefty sentence. Then, after heavy lobbying from Fred Hugi, she was transferred to the New Jersey Department of Corrections Clinton Correctional Facility for Women. The authorities apparently accepted Fred Hugi's concern that Downs was attempting to contact her surviving children, Christie and Danny.

Diane Downs was one determined lady, as she tried three more times to escape. Each was thwarted.

On 9 December 2008, at her first parole hearing, she reaffirmed her innocence saying, 'Over the years, I have told you and the rest of the world that a man shot me and my children. I have never changed my story.' However, Lane County District Attorney Douglas Harcleroad wrote to the parole board commenting in part, 'Downs continues to fabricate new versions of events under which the crimes occurred.' Then after three hours of interviews and a half hour of deliberation, she was denied parole.

On 10 December 2010 she made a second attempt to apply for parole, and still declared her innocence and that she didn't shoot her children. Again she was denied parole and the parole board voted to postpone her next hearing for 10 years, the longest deferral allowed, for reasons that included her failure to demonstrate understanding of what led to her crimes and her lack of remorse or empathy. And she now had to wait for another 10 years before she could apply again, by which time she would be 65 years old.

At the time of writing in 2020, Diane Downs was incarcerated in California and again eligible for parole in early 2021. It is unclear whether this latest application has been delayed by the COVID-19 pandemic, which Downs likened to Edgar Allan Poe's 1842 short story 'The Masque of the Red Death'. 'The red death had long devastated the country' where the story begins. 'No pestilence had ever been so fatal, or so hideous. Blood was its Avatar and its seal — the madness and the horror of blood.'

Whether this new development will make any difference is any one's guess.

7.

THE DROWNING TUB MURDERS: ANDREA YATES

'To the woman He (our Lord) said, "I will greatly multiply your
pain in childbirth, in pain you will bring forth children;
Yet your desire will be for your husband, and he will rule over you."'
— Genesis 3:16

Andrea Pia Yates (c. 2002)
PHOTOGRAPH COURTESY OF *HOUSTON CHRONICLE*

Parenting has a way of bringing out the best and the worst in people, and in this particular story, a mother's natural instincts to protect her children appeared to go awry. It seems unimaginable that a woman who is supposed to nourish, care for and love her babies would murder them. But sadly, here is a case where a mother took the lives of her five children in a deliberate, systematic way through drowning them.

The tragedy of this particular case is that it may have been averted if family or authorities had noted Andrea Yates's signs and symptoms and acted appropriately.

■

Andrea Pia Yates (nee Kennedy) was born in Hallsville, Texas on 2 July 1964. She was the youngest of the five children of Jutta Karin Koehler, a German immigrant, and Andrew Emmett Kennedy, whose parents were Irish immigrants. Andrea graduated from Milby High School in Houston in 1982. She was the class valedictorian (a student generally having the highest rank in a graduating class), captain of the swimming team and an officer in the National Honour Society. A good start in life.

Andrea completed a two-year pre-nursing course at the University of Houston, graduated from the University of Texas School of Nursing in Houston and began working as a registered nurse. It was during this time she met Russell ('Rusty') Yates, both 25 years old, at their apartment complex in Houston. Before meeting Rusty, Andrea was rather reserved, had suffered from depression and was recovering from a broken relationship.

Rusty Yates appeared to be a breath of fresh air and they eventually moved in together and spent a good deal of their time in prayer and religious study. On 17 April 1993 they were married and Andrea ceased working shortly after. Rusty had been a follower of the preacher Michael Peter Woroniecki, who was of the view that married couples should have as many children as possible. So, at their marriage ceremony it was no surprise that they told their guests they would 'seek to have as many babies as nature allowed'.

Well, Mrs Andrea Yates dutifully complied, and was pregnant with her first child in February 1994. The couple continued to have children and then moved to Texas with three boys, Noah, John and Paul. Following the birth of her fourth child, a boy, Luke, Andrea started showing postpartum depressive symptoms.

This was the first warning sign of things to come.

On 16 June 1999, Rusty came home from work and found his wife in a desperate state where she was chewing her fingers and shaking. The following day she tried to commit suicide from a drug overdose and was transferred to the Methodist Hospital psychiatric unit. She was kept under observation and prescribed an antidepressant and discharged on 24 June.

It was the beginning of a terrible tragedy.

Back home, Andrea didn't take her medication and began to self-mutilate. On 20 July, after putting a knife to her throat in an attempted suicide, she was again hospitalised in a catatonic state (inability to move normally) for 10 days. Her condition greatly improved after being treated with a series of drugs which included Haldol (haloperidol), an antipsychotic, and Rusty thought Andrea was like her former self when they met. She was discharged from hospital, however, in July 1999 she suffered a relapse resulting in a nervous breakdown. This was followed by two attempted suicides and further hospitalisations.

Dr Eileen Starbranch, warned the couple not to have any more children because she believed that having another baby would 'guarantee future psychotic depression' resulting in more psychotic behaviour. Despite this advice, Rusty still insisted Andrea try to have another child.

In the meantime, Andrea's family urged Rusty to buy a house instead of living in the now very cramped quarters of a modified bus. Fortunately, he then bought a nice home in a peaceful neighbourhood. Not surprisingly, Andrea's mental condition greatly improved and she returned to her past activities such as swimming and some socialising. She was taking her prescribed Haldol and also began to interact well with children.

It was the calm before the storm.

In March 2000 Andrea became pregnant with their fifth child and stopped taking her medication, including Haldol, which is used in the treatment of schizophrenia, mania in bipolar disorder, delirium, acute psychosis and hallucinations from alcohol withdrawal. On 30 November 2000, their first daughter, Mary, was born. Andrea appeared to be coping with the four boys, and now had a baby daughter to care for as well. She was taking her medication again, which no doubt helped her to cope with her situation.

However, on 12 March 2001, her father died and her mental health declined.

She promptly stopped taking her medication, began to mutilate herself and seemed unable to feed her baby daughter. Andrea was admitted to hospital on 1 April 2001, where she came under the care of a psychiatrist, Dr Mohammed Saeed, who treated her. She was later discharged, only to return again in May. Dr Saeed, now realising the situation, advised Rusty that Andrea needed supervision around the clock and not to leave her alone with the children.

Clearly, Andrea wasn't coping.

On 3 May 2001, Andrea in a 'near catatonic' state filled a bathtub in the middle of the day. Whether she was feeling suicidal and intended to drown herself at this point, was never ascertained. After this incident, the couple arranged to ensure that she and the children were watched over by either Rusty or his mother, Dora Yates, in the interest of their safety.

Unfortunately, it appeared Rusty Yates didn't really grasp the seriousness of the situation and changed Dr Saeed's plan. He began leaving his wife at home for an hour at time 'in an attempt to slowly build up her independence.' It proved to be a very poor strategy on Rusty Yates's part, with Dr Starbranch's earlier diagnosis now proving to be quite prophetic.

Then, on 20 June 2001 after Rusty left for work and before his mother arrived to help, Andrea put into action a terrible plan that had been brewing in her head for some time. She filled the bathtub with water, and then began systematically drowning her three youngest boys, Paul (three years), Luke (two) and John (five), laying each on her bed once they were dead. Then Mary (six months), her infant daughter, received the murderous treatment. Just as the awful act was completed, with the child's limp body floating in the water, Noah (seven) walked into the ghastly scene and asked his mother what was wrong with his sister.

The little boy suddenly realising the dangerous situation, ran and was quickly caught by his mother. He was shoved into the 'death tub' alongside the floating body of his sister, Mary. He fought desperately for life, coming up for air twice, but to no avail. Andrea held him down until he was dead. She took Mary's body to the bed and lay her in the arms of her brothers. Noah was left floating in the tub.

Andrea Yates then called the Houston police and confessed to what she had done. The law enforcement arrived a short time later and Andrea was escorted out of the house in a catatonic state in handcuffs.

It would have been an awful sight for Dora Yates as she pulled up in the driveway and learned from police what had happened to her five grandchildren whom she planned to look after that day.

Down at the police station, Andrea poured out the terrible confession and explained her actions saying she was a satanic mother and that her evil would pass onto her children, so punishment needed to be carried out. Dr Phillip Resnick visited Adrea twice during her imprisonment and came to the conclusion that she faced 'a cruel dilemma which turned upside down her sense of right and wrong' and that she believed by killing her children she was saving them from an eternity in hell.

The matter went to court the following year amid a great deal of controversy.

During the trial Andrea Yates's defence team entered a plea of not guilty by 'reason of insanity'. In March 2002, after a trial lasting three weeks, the jury rejected the insanity defence and found Andrea Yates guilty of capital murder. While the prosecution had sought the death penalty, the jury sought life in prison instead. Andrea Yates was sentenced to life imprisonment with an eligibility for parole in 2041, at the age of 77. However, the matter did not end there.

On 6 January 2005, a Texas Court of Appeals granted Andrea Yates a new trial. It was found that a Californian psychiatrist and prosecution witness, Dr Park Dietz, had given evidence that Andrea Yates was psychotic at the time of the offences, but knew right from wrong, and so she was not insane under Texas law. At the time Dr Dietz was a consultant for a television show, *Law & Order,* and it was suggested that Andrea Yates got the idea to drown her children from one of its episodes. It was later revealed by the show's producers that no such episode ever existed. The jury again rejected the death penalty and the life imprisonment sentence stood after learning of the false testimony.

Then at a second trial on 26 July 2006 a Houston jury of six men and six women found after three days of deliberation, that Andrea Yates was 'not guilty of murder by reason of insanity'. She was then committed to the North Texas State Hospital, Vernon Campus. In January 2007, she was sent to Kerrville State Hospital, a low-security mental hospital facility in Kerrville, Texas.

Postscript:
Rusty Yates divorced Andrea in 2004 and remarried in 2006. He has since divorced again.

Andrea Yates now spends hers days within the confines of Kerrville State Hospital for an indefinite stay. She has regularly waived a review of her status, the only way she is likely to be released.

Previously, in 2002, Andrea Yates's defence lawyer, George Parnham and his wife Mary Parnham, founded the Yates Memorial Fund to help raise awareness about postpartum depression. Mary Parnham is said to have told the *Houston Chronicle* that Andrea Yates is, '… thrilled to know that good things are being done for the legacy of her children, and that makes her happy.'

Given that response, maybe, just maybe, a little consideration, a little thought for others who have difficulties we might not be aware of, could have resulted in a different, happier outcome for this story.

8.

DEATH IN A DUCK POND:
THE RACHEL PFITZNER CASE

'Let us make that one point – that no child will be unwanted,
unloved, uncared for, or killed and thrown away.'
– Mother Teresa

Rachel Pfitzner in custody.

It was a warm spring day on 17 October 2007 when two young boys were riding their bikes in Mandurama reserve in the Sydney suburb of Ambarvale, New South Wales. It is a lovely spot to escape the hustle and bustle of city life and enjoy the tranquility of the lake and feed the ducks, along with many other birds that live in reserve. On this particular day, instead of the usual flotilla of ducks, the boys spotted a tartan suitcase floating among the reeds near the edge of the pond. On opening the suitcase the stench of death was overpowering. Inside was the body of a little boy wrapped in two plastic bags. He had clearly been the suitcase for some time.

What the boys had discovered in the floating suitcase was the body of two-year-old Dean Shillingsworth. The local police were contacted and set up a crime scene, which was followed up by the NSW Police Forensic Services Group. After an intensive investigation along with forensic evidence, the prime suspect was the boy's mother, Rachel Pfitzner, who lived in public housing estate in the nearby suburb of Rosemeadow. Rachel had a lengthy record of criminal offences which included assault and shoplifting. Dean was also known to family services and had at times been in the care of his Aboriginal parental grandmother, Ann Coffey. Previously, on 11 October, the NSW Department of Community Services (DOCS) had sought a Family Court warrant to place the toddler into the custody of his grandmother. Sadly, this didn't occur.

However, it didn't take too long for the police to realise that Dean's mother was the most likely offender and she was arrested and subsequently charged with Dean's murder. Bail wasn't sought and she was remanded into custody at Silverwater Women's Correctional Centre.

It was said that at the time of Dean's death the boy's father Paul Shillingsworth, an Aboriginal man, was in prison. Family members of Rachel Pfitzner said that she feared for her safety if Paul was released from prison. Whether this was true is difficult to determine. Also, Pfitzner's estranged father said that Rachel had three children, each from a different father. So, it appears Dean had an older half-sister and a younger half-brother.

In the meantime an impromptu shrine of flowers and toys was erected on the water's edge of the duck pond by the local community and a ceremony was held on 26 October at Mandurama Reserve in remembrance of Dean

Shillingsworth and he was accorded a traditional smoking ceremony. On 1 November 2007 Dean Shillingsworth's funeral was conducted in his hometown, Brewarrina, and was attended by over 300 family, friends and members of the community.

On 12 December 2007 Rachel Pfitzner appeared in court via audio-video link (AVL) from Silverwater Women's Correctional Centre. However, the case was adjourned without bail to allow a brief of evidence to be completed, the matter being put over to the following year.

On 28 October 2008 Rachel Pfitzner again appeared before court for a committal hearing. The prosecution told the court that when she was arrested she had told police that she shook her son by the cord of his hooded jumper and threw him onto the ground, after which he wet himself, made gurgling sounds and became unresponsive. Ms Pfitzner, believing him to be dead, then wrapped his body in plastic bags and placed him in the tartan suitcase.

Pfitzner's defence counsel, Ms Belinda Rigg, asked Dr Dianne Little, a forensic pathologist who had examined Dean Shillingsworth's body, whether his death was consistent with the account provided by his mother. Dr Little said the boy had been dead for up to a week and his body was too decomposed for the cause of death to be determined. However, the lack of bleeding on his brain, cast some doubt on the account that the child had been shaken to death. Dr Little added that it was a possibility the child may have been suffocated.

Ms Rigg pursued this line of questioning further asking, 'Is one of the possibilities in this case, as you see it, that death could have been caused by the placing of the child, who appeared to be deceased but wasn't, into the plastic bag and then into the suitcase?'

Dr Little replied, 'If he was *completely* unconscious but not yet dead, that's a possibility.'

Ms Pfitzner wept quietly as she sat in the dock. She was committed to stand trial and did not enter a plea.

Outside the court, Dean's grandfather Edmund Caban said they were relieved the matter was now going to trial commenting, 'That's the one thing I hope for.' But then added, 'We are getting there.'

In June 2009, Rachel Pfitzner pleaded guilty to manslaughter but not guilty to murder. The matter went before Justice Robert Hulme at the NSW Supreme Court on 18 August 2009 for the *murder* of Dean Shillingsworth.

Justice Hulme reiterated the various versions in which Dean had died: where he was shaken and then thrown to the ground, to the scenario where his mother choked him 'in a rage', by swinging him around by his jumper. He admitted that while Dean was asphyxiated, it was difficult to determine how this occurred. Determining reasons for the murder appeared almost as difficult. However, Rachel Pfitzner's troubled relationship with Dean's father, Paul Shillingsworth, provided a motive. He had allegedly threatened her and when she looked at the child, 'all I could see was Paul'. She then added, 'I just kept seeing his father and couldn't stop myself.'

The court learnt that Dean was supposed to be in the care of Paul Shillingsworth's mother, Mrs Ann Coffey. Unfortunately, his mother failed to return the boy after an access visit in July 2007 and she was 'on a real high to have him back'.

But the mother and son relationship deteriorated to such a point the toddler was punished for any childish misdemeanours, which were seen as deliberate disobedience. In reality, the child craved her affection, but she saw him as clingy,came to resent his presence and could no longer stand him touching her.

It was a terrible state of affairs. And it was clear that in the weeks before the murder Rachel Pfitzner was struggling to cope. But help *was* available. Rachel's mother had promised to look after Dean, while Mrs Coffey, his beloved grandmother, was taking legal action to take custody of the toddler.

In the meantime, on 3 October, Rachel told a social worker that she was unable to put up with Dean and 'just wanted him gone as soon as possible'.

Then, just eight days later, when the court ordered Dean to be taken into the custody of his grandmother, his second 'mum', the child lost his life.

Justice Hulme said in his concluding address, 'I am satisfied that she [Rachel Pfitzner] came to loathe Dean because he reminded her of his father, towards whom she held ambivalent feelings.' But his honour added,

'Dean was entitled to love, protection and nurture, but instead she took away his very life.'

Rachel Pfitzner was sentenced to a maximum of 25 years six months, with a non-parole period of at least 19 years and two months in jail.

This case was particularly tragic, as there was no shortage of people who would have given Dean Shillingsworth all the love the child craved, when his mother, Rachel Pfitzner, was unable. Something in the two-year-old boy triggered a rage within her. After weeks of mistreatment, he was eventually murdered.

But, amazingly, after the trial and the subsequent sentence, Rachel Pfitzner commented, 'Dean forgives me. He's safe now and with God.'

In July 2010 she appealed against the severity of the sentence. It was not successful.

9.

MOTHERS AND METHADONE: A DEADLY 'SEDATIVE'

'There's no one way to be a perfect mother
and a million ways to be a good one.'
– Jill Churchill

Methadone (Physeptone, Dolophine) was first synthesised by German chemists during World War II as a morphine substitute. The drug is a powerful analgesic used to relieve moderate to severe pain from a variety of sources including, trauma, surgery, heart attack and burns. The drug has also been used to treat the pain in cases of terminal cancer, where it eases the suffering and provides a feeling of euphoria and peace; very desirable outcomes for the terminally ill. Also, it is more reliable than morphine when given orally (by mouth).

However, unlike morphine, methadone produces a marked sedative effect and with repeated doses can result in drug build-up (accumulation). This is due to its rather long half-life of 15 to 55 hours (average 25 hours) – morphine is only 2.5 hours – with resultant toxic effects. The drug has proven useful as a direct substitute for opiate (heroin) users to help them minimise drug usage before withdrawal symptoms develop, and has been used for some time for addicts to control their habit. Hence, the use of the drug in various rehabilitation programs to wean heroin addicts off their habit.

Since the inception of methadone maintenance clinics in the late 1960s, accidental poisoning (and in some cases, deliberate poisoning) of children with methadone has been reported in the literature and the news media for example: 'Drug Threat to Children', 'Mum Gave Baby Methadone'.

Awful outcomes, with awful headlines.

■

The toxic effects of the methadone are more likely to occur in naive users before any tolerance has developed. For a relatively naive user, the starting dose is initially 10–20 milligrams (mg) per day, rising to a maintenance range of 30–50 mg per day (maximum 80 mg/day), with an average range of 30–40 mg per day. Aside from tablets (Physeptone, Dolophine), methadone is commonly supplied to addicts on a program in the form of an orange-flavoured syrup containing 5 mg/ml of the drug, which can be attractive to young children.

Methadone does not exert its full effects immediately after ingestion, and so it is possible to take a large dose without any immediate perception by the user of a life-threatening intoxication. There is often a time gap of several hours between taking the drug and eventual collapse – 'the drug isn't working'. So another dose is ingested, resulting in deep sedation and breathing difficulties, which steadily get worse depending upon how much was taken, with a possible fatal outcome. Unfortunately, 'methadone mums' (female heroin addicts undergoing therapy, with kids) have used the drug for its sedative effects on their youngsters for various reasons, as these cases illustrate:

The first case involved an apparently healthy, happy 18-month-old boy who spent the last day of his life playing on the floor of his parents' unit. However, his playing area was like no other – empty methadone bottles and syringes were left scattered around the unit and young Brent was apparently allowed to play with the syringe barrels 'like a toy'. The child was living in a world where both his parents, mum, Heather Davies and his dad, Michael Partridge, and another couple Peter and Donna Young, who were all heroin addicts, attending a methadone clinic, supposedly, to kick the habit. Heather apparently, supplemented her income through prostitution.

It had been a busy night with one client after another coming into the brothel. Heather and Donna were out all night working as prostitutes, before returning to their shared unit in the wee small hours of the morning at about 5 am in November 1995.

Heather's baby boy of 18 months was experiencing the arrival of his first teeth, and this was causing him some discomfort, aside from a viral infection. The baby boy, Brent, was restless, and Heather apparently gave him '… a tiny little bit' of methadone to soothe his teething pains, and may well have taken some herself, as both mum and her baby then fell asleep in the lounge chair, the baby lying stomach down on his mother's lap. Hours passed, and Heather eventually awoke at 1 pm and placed the child on a lounge chair, where he apparently appeared to be still asleep. Unfortunately, he wasn't. He was in a deep drug-induced coma. Brent's father Michael Partridge went to place him into his cot in the bedroom at about 3 pm, when he noticed that he was not moving and had turned blue in complexion. An ambulance was called, along with the police, who arrived a short time later. The residence was in a state of disarray and the bedroom very untidy, with dirty clothes and other items strewn around the floor, cot and bed of the residence. The ambulance arrived at about 3.20 pm and found that the child had been dead for some hours. It was later ascertained that baby Brent Partridge had been dead for up to six hours before Heather had realised anything was wrong.

A blood sample taken from the deceased child at post-mortem was found to contain methadone 0.5 milligrams per litre. A high level even for an adult, let alone a toddler. The child's liver was found to contain 0.71 milligram per kilogram and the stomach contents (weighing about 27 grams) were found to contain 22 mg/kg of methadone (or about 0.6 mg). The level of methadone found in the toddler's blood was more than enough to result in the death of a child of this age.

There the matter lay, until it was taken to Glebe Coroner's Court in February 2003, to try to answer the questions surrounding baby Brent's tragic death. In particular, how did the deadly drug get into his body? There initially, appeared to be two likely scenarios, either one or both parents administered it in an effort to sedate him or somehow, the toddler found some methadone syrup in a container lying on the floor. 'Take away' methadone is usually provided as an orange-flavoured syrup containing 5 milligrams per millilitre of the drug.

I estimated that for an infant weighing 18 kilograms, a minimum dosage of 24 to 28 milligrams (or 5–6 ml, about a teaspoon) would have had to have been taken to achieve the methadone blood level found. Could the infant have taken the drug himself? It seemed unlikely in my view.

Another two years passed. In February 2005 Brent Partridge's stood trial in the New South Wales Supreme Court in Darlinghurst charged with manslaughter. What had happened in the meantime?

In an unusual turn of events, Heather Davies and Michael Partridge stood trial before a judge alone, namely Justice David Kirby, with no jury.

The Crown prosecutor, Richard Herps, in making his opening remarks, told the court that both the accused were on a methadone program at the time of the toddler's death and had taken some of the drug that morning.

He further told the court that the prosecution would allege that the child was either given the methadone as a sedative or the child consumed the drug himself while his parents were asleep.

The defence solicitor, Phil Gibson, took the latter position. He was aided by the fact that a 1997 report describing the child's death through methadone intoxication had sat in the coroner's court for years, while recordings, police notes and methadone exhibits had been destroyed. These matters were raised by his honour. Unfortunately, I hadn't requested that the boy's hair be tested for methadone. If the drug was present, this would have been very useful information to determine whether the methadone ingestion was a one off or a chronic ingestion, which would have indicated neglect of the child.

Ms Davies apparently confessed to her brother Michael Ford, several weeks after Brent's death, that she deliberately gave him methadone. According to a statement Mr Ford made to police, the conversation apparently went like this:

'I want to talk to you about Brent.'

'What do you want to tell me?' he asked.

'He must have licked that methadone off a spoon,' Heather replied.

'We are talking about an 18-month-old baby darling, to my mind that would be impossible. Did you give it to him?'

Sobbing, Holly then said to her brother, 'I didn't think the little bit that I gave him would've killed him. I just wanted to ease the pain that he was in.'

Well, that certainly was achieved. More importantly, Mr Ford admitted that his sister was intoxicated at the time of the confession. Unfortunately, Mr Ford had since died from cancer and so could not be cross-examined on this issue. However, the prosecution said Mr Ford's account supported the evidence given by Kathryn Adams, who has a daughter with one of Holly Davies' brothers, who said that she had given methadone to toddler Brent for teething pain.

Justice Kirby found that the prosecution failed to produce enough evidence that methadone was deliberately given to the child or that there was criminal negligence by Davies or the boy's father, Partridge. Therefore, there was insufficient evidence for a conviction over the death of Brent

Partridge and so they were cleared over the child's methadone death.

Outside the court, Davies' solicitor Phil Gibson said his client was relieved.

This was hardly surprising, since she had admitted much earlier that she had given him '… a tiny little bit'. I guess, a teaspoon or more may be a small amount to an addict, but proved to be a fatal amount for a toddler.

As Ms Davies' solicitor said, 'It is still a tragedy, and Holly has to live with the tragedy of Brent's death every day.'

Brent would have been approaching his 25th birthday (at the time of writing in 2020), and if this tragedy had not occurred, he had his whole life ahead of him but for 'a tiny bit [of methadone]' to ease teething pain.

■

Bermagui is a relaxed, attractive fishing and surfing village on the far south coast of New South Wales. Writer and big-game fisherman Zane Grey placed Bermagui on the global calendar and established the birthplace of game fishing for black marlin and yellowfin tuna in the 1930s, which has continued today. The Sapphire Coast is a wonderful tourist destination and not a place you would expect the sort of problems that unfolded in this second case.

Young Tyson Gray-McGregor was a happy, healthy four-year-old boy who lived with his mother Naomi Gray and his nine-year-old sister, Kelli, in Bermagui. Naomi, being a single mum, found things difficult and found friendship in the form of Alan Thornton, who was from another south coast town of Moruya. The friendship developed, and Alan was invited to stay the night at Naomi's home on 17 January 2005. It turned out that Alan Thornton was on a local methadone program for opiate (heroin) dependency problems. At that time his daily dosage was 26 millilitres of methadone syrup supplied at a strength of 5 milligrams per millilitre, giving an effective daily dose of 130 milligrams of methadone. A fairly strong dosage, indicating he was in the early stage of his methadone program.

But, the kids were excited, 'Uncle Alan is staying over!' and so could not sleep.

Tyson in particular was more restless and his mother and 'Uncle' Alan were having difficulty in getting him to settle and go to sleep. This apparently posed some problems, as both children were sleeping in the same bedroom. At about 10.30 pm Tyson was apparently still wide awake and no doubt getting him to settle was discussed, including giving him some methadone syrup in a drink to get him to go to sleep.

As it had been a late night, both Naomi Gray and Alan Thornton had slept in until about 9.45 am. Naomi awoke, and not hearing the children playing, which she thought unusual, she went into the children's bedroom. She saw both children still lying in their respective beds and thought they were both still asleep. She then went over to check Tyson and saw he was blue around the lips and cold to touch. He was apparently dead, and had been dead for some hours as post-mortem lividity and rigor mortis had already set in. She screamed out to Alan and he came running into the room. Attempts at CPR (cardiopulmonary resuscitation) were fruitless and the police and ambulance were called. Later, Tyson's little body was collected and taken for post-mortem to determine the cause of his death.

About two weeks later, Alan Thornton admitted to a witness before the child's funeral that he put some methadone in a cordial given to Tyson to make him settle, and '… that he must have put in too much'. The addition of the methadone to the child's drink was done with the knowledge and consent of his mother.

A blood sample taken from the deceased child at post-mortem was found to contain methadone 0.3 milligrams per litre. This level was again more than enough to result in the death of a child of this age. In addition, 1.3 milligrams of methadone was found in his bile, indicating some time had elapsed prior to his death.

Both Naomi Gray and Alan Thornton were apparently remorseful, and due to a drug overdose were unable to attend Tyson's funeral. A deliberate overdose of methadone? In any case, both parties fortunately recovered in hospital and were able to attend court.

The drug was apparently given to the child to 'help make him sleep' and it certainly achieved that – a deadly sedative. In opposing bail, police told the court they had evidence that Thornton had given Tyson methadone in a cordial drink because 'He would not settle [sleep] for the night.' Magistrate David Helipern refused Thornton bail, but released Naomi Gray on the condition she reported to police at Bermagui three times a week.

I attended court at Bega and advised legal counsel in the matter. The level of methadone that was present in Tyson's blood was more than sufficient to result in the death of the child. It appeared that a minimum of just over half a teaspoon of methadone syrup had been administered to the child, assuming the original mixture was at the usual concentration of methadone, 5 milligrams per millilitre. Given the level of the drug was present in the child's bile, it is likely more of the drug had been given to 'settle him' with fatal results.

Tyson's mother Naomi Gray received a 21-month suspended jail sentence when she was sentenced before Justice McLoughlin in Bega Court on 8 March 2007. The suspension was conditional that she entered into a good behaviour bond and be under the directions of her parole officer at all times for the duration of the bond. Alan Thornton had previously pleaded guilty to manslaughter in connection with the boy's death and received a six-year sentence with a non-parole period of four years.

■

Campbelltown is an outer western suburb of Sydney and the city derives its name from Elizabeth Campbell, the wife of the former Governor of New South Wales, Lachlan Macquarie. It was originally called Campbell-Town, and the name was later simplified to the present Campbelltown. It is also notable for an incident that, according to folklore, occurred in 1826 when a local farmer, Frederick Fisher, disappeared and his ghost later appearing sitting on a fence rail over a creek just south of the town. Eerily, the apparition pointed to the site where his body was later found. Due to this incident, the Fisher's Ghost Festival is held each November in Campbelltown.

Fortunately, in this third case I didn't encounter any apparitions. But sadly, it still involved another death of an infant child – also due to methadone.

It was a cool, early morning at about 5 am on 23 August 2006, when Sheila Kelly was apparently breastfeeding her three-week-old daughter Michelle Kelly in the rear room of their house. A very natural thing to do with a newborn baby. Unfortunately, this morning was going to be very different, as the baby began to choke. She started to turn blue and stopped breathing for no apparent reason. Sheila, realising what was happening to her baby, began screaming, 'My baby, my baby, my baby,' and woke her partner Lee Townsend who was sleeping in the lounge room. Upon hearing her screams, Lee ran to the rear room where Sheila had been feeding their child.

He noticed a wet patch around the baby's head and some blood coming from the child's nose. This was odd and very disturbing. And why after just breast feeding? The 000 number was promptly called for an ambulance to attend. The ambulance arrived a short time later and attempted to resuscitate the baby. At about 5.40 am ambulance officers took the baby and her mother to Campbelltown Hospital. At 5.44 am the ambulance arrived at the hospital and handed the baby to hospital staff. Intensive efforts were made by hospital staff to resuscitate the baby, but they were unsuccessful. At 5.56 am baby Michelle was declared dead by a doctor at Campbelltown Hospital. However, Sheila apparently could not accept that her baby daughter was dead. When police arrived at Campbelltown Hospital they found her sitting in a chair holding the dead baby in her left arm. Sheila had her head resting on a bed and was crying. Her baby was wrapped in a yellow blanket and a tube was still in her mouth from earlier resuscitation attempts. She remained sitting, holding the baby, and was continually crying and talking to the baby, asking her to wake up. Eventually, Sheila stood up and placed her baby in a cot beside her and walked out of the room.

At 12.00 pm a government contractor arrived and removed the baby's body, which was then taken to the Westmead Hospital Forensic Medicine section.

A blood sample taken from the deceased child at post-mortem was found to contain methadone 0.1 milligrams per litre. This level was again more than enough to result in the death of a child of this age. In addition, 0.4 milligrams per kilogram of methadone was found in her liver, indicating some time had elapsed prior to her death. Methadone was also detected in her stomach contents. Obviously, the baby had taken the drug orally.

The therapeutic range for methadone in adults is given as 0.05–

1.0 milligrams per litre. However, death may occur at low blood levels and the level detected in baby Michelle's blood was 0.1 milligrams per litre – given her age, more than enough to seriously depress her central nervous system to the extent of causing her death.

The risks of methadone to children and naive users have been well documented, but little action appears to have been taken over the years to reduce these dreadful casualties. Little baby Michelle appeared to be yet another casualty, and the level appeared far too high to be a carry-over from breast milk.

The matter eventually went before the coroner at Westmead, who found that there was insufficient evidence that methadone was deliberately given to the child or that there was criminal negligence by Ms Kelly. Astonishingly, an interstate expert suggested the methadone came from the mother's milk. This observation was not and has not been supported by the scientific literature. After much legal argument the coroner returned an open finding, as the manner in which the baby had ingested the methadone could not be determined with any degree of certainty. This was yet another case where a beautiful child was lost to methadone intoxication.

◼

A fourth case involving methadone appeared much more insidious.

A six-year-old girl was found dead at the foot of her mother's bed. The household consisted of the six-year-old, her mother, her mother's de-facto husband and his two children. The mother stated that on the Friday (two days prior to her death), her six-year-old daughter had flu-like symptoms and had vomited on a number of occasions. The mother gave her some Dimetapp (brompheniramine and phenylephrine) and Dymadon (paracetamol). On the surface, appropriate treatment.

The following day (Saturday), she was given some more Dimetapp and fell asleep. When she woke she vomited again. Around 1.30 am on Sunday, the child was asleep in her mother's bed, she was woken and taken to her own bed.

However around 3 am, the six-year-old asked her mother for some water and more Dimetapp. According to her mother she was very alert. The child then returned to her bed. Around 7 am on Sunday, the mother woke to find her daughter asleep at the foot of her bed and the mother said she was sleeping and breathing normally. At 9 am the defacto partner checked on the child and found she had no movement and was not breathing.

An ambulance was called and a doctor also attended and found the child was cyanosed, cold, had no pulse and was in asystole (no cardiac activity). The mother stated she had been on methadone for about 12 years and she picked up takeaway doses of methadone (35 mg) from her pharmacy. It was supplied in small brown bottles with a white cap under the trade name, Biodone.

She allegedly had her prescriptions faxed to her by her doctor (which was very unusual). In the meantime, investigating police found some 28 bottles of various sizes containing methadone in the house, including four 500 ml bottles of Biodone (methadone syrup) some with the tamper-proof manufacturer's seal still intact, two full 250 ml bottles and various smaller bottles. A total of over 3 litres! The mother's explanation was she was 'storing a bit' because she was on a pension. (Methadone would never be dispensed to a patient in such commercial quantities in Australia.)

Some syringes were also found in the house containing traces of methadone.

But an interesting finding was a small, brown, unlabelled bottle with a white pump cap which was subsequently found to contain a solution of lignocaine. The significance of this find would be apparent later in the investigation, as ambulance officers who attended to the dead child did not administer the drug. (Lignocaine aside from being a local anaesthetic is used to treat cardiac arrhythmias.)

The toxicology results of a femoral blood sample taken from the six-year old deceased girl was found to have present methadone of 0.7 mg/L and lignocaine <0.1 mg/L. The stomach contents also indicated the presence of methadone (no level indicated), as did the liver (1.5 mg/kg). Later the deceased's hair sample was analysed and methadone was found to be present in each of seventeen 2 cm segments of hair. Clearly a chronic exposure to the drug.

When reinterviewed the mother of the child indicated the small brown

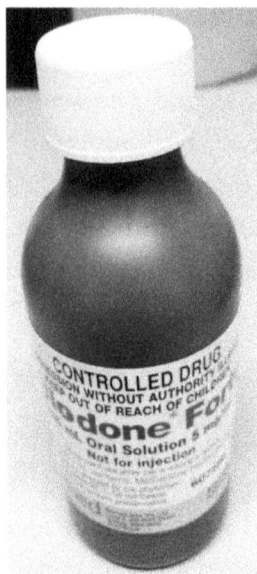
A typical Biodone syrup preparation.

bottle with the white pump cap contained lignocaine, which she used because the Biodone had a very unpleasant taste. The lignocaine spray was apparently used to 'deaden' (anaesthetise) the taste buds of the tongue. While police were investigating the suspicious death of the six-year-old, the mother administered some Dimetapp to the two stepchildren. The older 12-year-old later told police the mother usually gave them Dimetapp via a syringe. On this occasion (after the death of the six-year-old) when she was given the Dimetapp, it did not taste like Dimetapp. Both she and her younger sibling vomited after being given the medication and were later taken to hospital suffering from the effects of methadone. They were both found to have methadone in their blood (<0.1 mg/L).

Was this a clever cover-up?

The mother then claimed she realised she must have given the same Dimetapp to her daughter and she realised it was Biodone in the bottle. The de-facto partner did not use methadone but he was allegedly a user of prescribed dexamphetamine. He stated to police that the mother put methadone in various bottles and had them in various places around the house.

At court it was alleged the mother had administered the deceased child some methadone, allegedly contained in a Dimetapp bottle, and it was alleged the lignocaine was given to the child so that she would not react to the bitter taste of the drug (real Dimetapp has a very pleasant sweet taste which most children like). The jury of eight women and four men were told the deceased girl had methadone in all segments of her hair, which an expert in hair analysis said indicated long term administration of methadone.

I had to agree.

Also, she had a fatal level of methadone in her blood. However, contrary to earlier evidence, at the trial, the hair expert suggested the findings in the hair may have resulted from vomit on the hair or close contact with the sweat from the mother's skin when she slept in her mother's bed. I found this conclusion quite strange and most unlikely. Mainly, because hair samples are washed with solvents such as alcohol before being subject to analysis. This procedure effectively removes any extraneous drug substances from the exterior of the hair fibres.

The de-facto partner, contrary to his earlier statement to police, stated he put the methadone into the Dimetapp box without the mother's knowledge.

The jury found the mother not guilty of manslaughter and not guilty of supplying a prohibited drug. As such, she was cleared of killing her six-year-old daughter with a methadone overdose and walked free from court.

However, there was much the jury wasn't told as the newspapers headlines revealed for example:

Daily Telegraph headline 'What the Jury Didn't Know'.

The mother had a history of prostitution and drug offences dating back two decades and had a history with the Department of Community Services in relation to neglect of children in her care, including one child being admitted to hospital in an intoxicated state.

The natural father of the deceased child indicated he would sue the de-facto partner for the administration of methadone to his child and he also indicated he wanted an inquiry into the evidence given in relation to the hair analysis and the contradictory evidence of the expert.

Unfortunately, these cases are typical of the many encountered over the years, and illustrate the danger associated with takeaway methadone preparations particularly, for small children of parents undergoing treatment. The delay in seeking help in the majority of the cases appeared to be related to the parents' 'total unawareness of the danger inherent in methadone for their child until drowsiness and decreased respiration became quite apparent'. Therefore, it is essential that strict legislative safety measures be implemented to eliminate this safety hazard for children of patients on a methadone maintenance program.

One wonders how many more children will die from this drug before effective controls are put into practice.

10.

DEATH OF INNOCENCE:
THE KRISTI ANNE ABRAHAMS CASE

'The killing of innocent people is always wrong.'
– Bianca Jagger

Kristi Anne Abrahams.
PHOTOGRAPH COURTESY OF THE COURIER-MAIL

This story begins in the outer western suburb of Sydney, Mount Druitt. The area was named after Major George Druitt, who was allocated a large land grant by Governor Lachlan Macquarie, and it is now part of the Greater Western region of Sydney.

Unfortunately, Mount Druitt has been considered one of the main hotspots for a variety of crimes ranging from robbery and drug offences to murder. It was here that Kristi Anne Abrahams spent her childhood with her violent and alcoholic father, who subsequently spent large periods of his life in custody. Then at the age of 10, she made the terrible discovery of her dead mother in the bedroom of their home. With no parents to look after her, Kristi spent many years in and out of foster care. A tough start for any child.

Kristi was a damaged person, a potential damaging mother, which ultimately led to the pointless abuse and murder of yet another vulnerable and defenceless child. This is what happened to Kiesha Weippeart, the six-year-old who was murdered by her mother, Kristi Anne Abrahams, on 18 July 2010, after years of abuse.

Another failure of the system.

■

It was about 8 am on a wet and warm morning of 22 April 2011 that after months of planning, police conducted an intensive search of wooded land off Stoney Creek Road at Shalvey in Sydney's west. They eventually found a shallow grave site with skeletal remains, along with a burnt-out suitcase. Police believed that they had found the body of the missing little girl, Kiesha Weippeart. However, a police spokesperson said, 'The remains, which have yet to be positively identified, will be taken to Glebe Morgue for forensic examination.' Adding, 'A post-mortem will also be conducted to establish the cause of death.'

The previous year, on 3 August 2010, Kristi Anne Abrahams reported that her daughter Kiesha Weippeart was missing. In a tearful and heart-wrenching encounter before television cameras, the grief-stricken 27-year-old mother pleaded for her daughter's return, 'If anyone has seen her can they please contact the police. She's beautiful …'

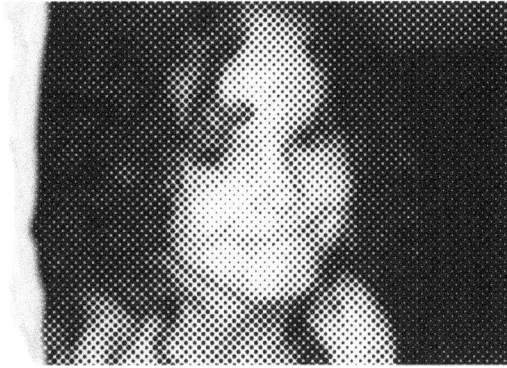

Kiesha Weippeart. SOURCE: *THE GUARDIAN*

Indeed, she was a beautiful child.

The emotional pleas by Ms Abrahams for help to find her daughter initiated a major search by hundreds of police and SES volunteers. Many locals held candlelit vigils outside the little girl's Mt Druitt home where a makeshift tribute was made of flowers, soft toys and heartfelt messages. Lovely gestures from many decent parents who empathised with the loss of a child.

But even then, things didn't seem quite right.

Ms Abrahams had called triple-0 two days before, explaining to the police operator that she had been woken at 9.30 am on Sunday morning to discover her daughter was missing. However, within 24 hours police investigations revealed that the cute, curly-haired little girl with the impish grin hadn't been seen at school or been seen by anybody else *since that July*.

Clearly, something was amiss and police were suspicious.

In the meantime, a task force named Strike Force Jarocin was set up to investigate the disappearance of Kiesha. Suspicions soon focused on Kristi Abrahams and her live-in boyfriend, Robert Smith. A meticulously planned, nine-month police investigation, which included undercover officers and hidden surveillance cameras, eventually led to a confession from Robert Smith, and the discovery of Kiesha's remains in a shallow bushland grave in Shalvey. Her little body exhibited wounds consistent with long-term abuse and serious blunt-force trauma, which indicated she had met her end by being thrown into the ground or slammed against a hard object, such as a wall.

Robert Smith and Kristi Abrahams were arrested in a laneway in Freya Street, Shalvey, shortly after Kiesha's makeshift grave was located in April 2011, eight months after she was reported missing. They were taken to Mt Druitt police station and questioned by detectives. The pair were later formally charged with the murder of the little girl. It would have been Kiesha's seventh birthday.

Amazingly, Robert Smith, 33, claimed he had been physically abused by Kristi Abrahams, and pleaded guilty to manslaughter and to being an accessory to murder. Well, the latter stuck. He had sealed his fate.

Justice Megan Latham, found that he had made a 'simple and cowardly' decision to do nothing when Kiesha was seriously assaulted by her mother and then took a lead role in disposing of her body in a suitcase and dousing it with petrol before setting it alight. Smith was sentenced to 16 years in jail with a non-parole period of 12 years.

The same tactic was taken by Kristi Abrahams, now 30 years old, who admitted to Kiesha's manslaughter. Given the evidence presented, not surprisingly, the prosecution rejected her plea, forcing her to proceed to trial for murder.

The matter went before Justice Ian Harrison at the NSW Supreme Court on 18 July 2013. In sentencing her for the murder of her 'defenceless six-year-old daughter', he described Ms Abrahams as 'an inevitable product of entrenched intergenerational failures'.

Justice Harrison continued, 'As anyone knows, the burdensome responsibilities of parenthood are not bestowed only on those who are capable of meeting them. [Ms] Abrahams was patently ill equipped for the role and probably equally unable to recognise it.'

Earlier, the court had heard that Kristi Abrahams, who at the tender age of 10 found her mother dead, had endured a life of abuse and neglect as a child, and was also hampered by an intellectual disability. Curiously, the man she blamed for her early life of pain, her father, was the very person she wanted to look after Kiesha when she said, 'I can't f***ing handle the kid anymore.'

Justice Harrison said that while he couldn't be satisfied that Ms Abrahams intended to kill her six-year-old daughter, or whether she was responsible for the sustained abuse of Kiesha, she had meant to seriously injure her.

Ms Abrahams said, upon her guilty plea, that she gave Kiesha 'a little nudge' after a struggle to put her pyjamas on at bedtime. This was not consistent with medical evidence and not accepted by the Crown.

A post-mortem of Kiesha's body by Dr Matthew Orde revealed serious physical abuse, both in the past and more recently. An examination of her teeth revealed that she had received as many as five blows to the jaw before she died. Clearly at odds with a 'nudge' causing the child to hit her head on a bed.

Justice Harrison said, 'How Kiesha died is not known to me and I have been unable to provide a satisfactory version to replace it.'

Determing reasons for the murder appeared almost as difficult. However, Kristi Abraham's troubled relationship with Kiesha's father, Christopher Weippeart, may have provided a motive for the abuse to the child. As Kristi Abrahams admitted, she was 'annoyed' by Kiesha's resemblance to her biological father.

Justice Harrison before passing sentence said, '… the murder of a vulnerable and defenceless child in her care was in the mid-range of seriousness' and believed she was unlikely to offend. Ms Abrahams was then told to stand and learn her fate. He further commented, 'Retribution and mercy are important in equal measure.'

Kristi Abrahams was then given a sentence of 21 years and six months, along with an additional 18 months for 'interfering with a corpse'. With the two penalties combined, she had been sentenced to a minimum non-parole period of 16 years. With time already served, Ms Abrahams will be eligible for parole in 2027.

As she was led away to serve her sentence, the packed Supreme Court gallery erupted with jeers from a large group of Kiesha's supporters yelling, 'Rot in hell, putrid dog.'

But one supporter commented quite pointedly, 'Does having a bad upbringing and abuse give you the right to go and take people's lives? She

[Abrahams] knew what she was doing. It's just a cop-out. Kiesha was killed by a cold-blooded murderer.'

Sadly, many people saw signs that Kiesha was in danger – including DOCS (Department of Community Services) – from a violent mother. Another failure of the system designed to protect the vulnerable.

The officer-in-charge of the investigation into Kiesha Weippeart's death, Detective Inspector Russell Oxford, declined to be drawn into commenting about the sentence handed down, but said, 'If nothing else comes out of today, we should all take stock of where we are in this world and go home and hug our kids.'

As someone added, 'May Kiesha rest in peace.'

A fitting epitaph for a young and vulnerable child.

11.

THE 'BLACK WIDOW':
THE KERRY FORREST CASE

'Bill … Have a nice rest.'
– Kerry Forrest

Kerry Forrest in custody.
SOURCE: *DAILY MAIL.*

As a forensic investigator, from time to time, I've been involved in cases of extraordinary human treachery that have sometimes left me quite speechless. This one was exceptional. Here was a case where a woman poisoned her trusting elderly friend and subsequently lover with an overdose of morphine for purely financial gain.

■

Kerry Forrest (nee McGregor) was born on 20 September 1959 to a lower-middle-class family. At 15 years of age, she set out on her life of crime with several stealing charges, appearing before Minda Children's Court Central, where she was committed to six months institutional care for each offence. She then 'graduated' with a false pretences charge and appeared before Albion Street Children's Court, where she was fingerprinted and spent further time in institutional care. From then on, there was a continuous string of charges, ranging from stealing from dwellings to various fraudulent acts, with appearances before courts such as Parramatta Petty Sessions, and later, Windsor Court of Petty Sessions. In addition, she committed a number of traffic offences, including displaying a misleading registration label.

She subsequently changed her surname to Jewel, and it stayed that way until she met Wayne John Forrest, whom she married after getting out of jail, when she took on the name Kerry Forrest. They had two daughters, Kisha and Kara, but normal domestic life was never on the cards, and a number of scams, including several fictitious assaults for compensation, eventually led to divorce and Wayne Forrest remarrying his first wife, Gail.

But Kerry was only just getting started. The stage was now set for the big one – a financial venture that was to dupe William 'Bill' Adamson, a recently widowed war veteran. He was 84 and his 90-year-old wife, Beryl, had passed away in September 2009 from Alzheimer's disease.

His first contact with Kerry had been in 2002, on the internet, where he ran a business called Australian Rain Saver. Kerry expressed interest in purchasing one of the products on offer, and over the years, she told Bill that she was 'going through a bit of a hard time with her husband'. They struck up a friendship and he would ring and ask if she was alright. At that stage, the relationship was purely platonic with no other involvement.

Prior to Beryl's death, Bill had employed two health care workers to look after her; one was a qualified nurse and the other was a carer. After she died, they were no longer needed, but he still wanted a companion to cook his meals, wash his clothes, do some ironing and carry out some housework, so he advertised the position through Seek, an employment agency. At the same time, Kerry wanted to leave her allegedly abusive husband and was searching for work. She saw Bill's advertisement for a live-in carer, and noting that appropriate qualifications weren't considered necessary, as the duties were considered purely domestic with no medical issues involved, she jumped at the opportunity, and Bill was happy to welcome her aboard the 'good ship Adamson'.

It appeared to be a mutually agreeable arrangement and Kerry promptly moved into the Kareela property, where she was provided with a self-contained granny flat. They settled into a routine, with Kerry apparently also receiving some government benefits as a carer to Bill.

Before long, a joint bank account was set up, a strong indication that the relationship was clearly becoming more intimate than that of employer and employee, and then Bill put his house up for sale. It was never clear why, except maybe for him to have sufficient money to buy a waterfront property. His business was based in the Kareela house and it had been home for him and Beryl for many years. It was not far from Oyster Bay, various parklands and many other local facilities. All in all, it was a very nice location in south Sydney.

Not surprisingly, given the location and the Sydney property boom at the time, the property sold quickly. So quickly, in fact, that Bill and Kerry had to find alternative accommodation in a hurry and storage for the furniture and various household goods. Some were even stored in an adjoining neighbour's property.

Apparently, the plan, or at least what Bill, a former realtor and property developer thought it was, was to build a house on a plot of land that Kerry owned in Bundanoon, a town in the Southern Highlands, south of Sydney. Bill's house sold for $690,000, leaving a profit of $319,000. That was duly deposited into their joint account, which was subsequently transferred to Kerry's account on 12 April 2010.

They packed their immediate possessions, along with Bill's medications, into the boot of a 1993 Lexus sedan and headed off to Campbelltown, an outer suburb of Sydney, to stay at the Maclin Lodge Motel, which Kerry had previously booked because it was close to her daughter, Kara, who lived in nearby Camden. The room was well appointed, containing two queen-sized beds and a large flat-screen television but, curiously, Kerry had only booked it for a week and paid cash up front at $110 a night plus a further $50 for the key, a total of $820.

At 6.35 pm on the evening of Monday 12 April 2010, Bill and Kerry moved into room 58. The first couple of days were uneventful, with Kerry going to Woolworths to get some hot chicken and other food items. Then on the evening of 14 April, Bill decided to go to bed early, as he was very tired, and he began to snore quite heavily. While he slept, Kerry placed a 'Do Not Disturb' sign on the door, later giving as a reason the fact that a woman had 'barged in' while she and Bill had still been asleep in their beds the previous day. On the morning of 15 April 2010 she left Bill in the room, but not before placing a note, written on Maclin Lodge Motel paper, behind a plastic jug:

Bill,

Gone to MOVIES & SHOPS & to do all the things you wanted me to do.

Will be home very late.

I will try to be very quiet.

Have a nice rest.

Love Kerry

When she returned in the early hours of Friday 16 April 2010 Bill was still lying in the same position on the bed. It was plain that he was dead and had been for some time. Kerry then contacted Dr Tan Mao, the family doctor, hoping that she would come to the motel room, examine Bill, pronounce him dead and issue a death certificate, thus avoiding a police investigation. But, unfortunately for Kerry, Dr Mao had other commitments and said she couldn't go to the motel, whereupon Kerry, quite inexplicably, drove to the doctor to collect Bill's medical records. She then returned to the motel and later telephoned 000 at about 10.50 pm. The police arrived soon after, and the stench of death was only too apparent.

A crime scene was set up and various items and medications were photographed before being removed for later forensic examination. Bill's body, after being photographed, was taken to the Glebe mortuary. Meanwhile, Kerry went to Campbelltown police station and was interviewed by ERISP (Electronically Recorded Interview of a Suspected Person).

Although she wasn't under arrest, she was interviewed for some hours and asked various questions as to what had led to Bill's death. She was very keen to distance herself from it, saying that she'd got back Friday afternoon at about 4 pm and found him 'stone cold' and believed he'd died in his sleep from 'extreme exhaustion'. However, she'd waited until nearly 11 pm before calling the police. That irregularity was further explored during the ERISP, but she was insistent that everything had been normal and that 'he just fell asleep with the telly on' while he was in bed and that she'd previously gone out to purchase food.

Her stories were starting to become inconsistent and further questions were asked.

'Do you know how he died?'

'In his sleep.'

'Do you know what may have caused him to die?'

'I have no idea.'

'Were you involved in his death in any way?'

'No.'

The interview terminated at 2.20 am and Kerry was allowed to head back to the motel, which she checked out of the following day, preferring to stay with her daughter, Kara.

She now had a sizeable bank account of over $300,000, and no doubt looked forward to spending it. However, she had a serious gambling habit, and within three months, she'd gambled the lot away on poker machines. Gambling, unlike drinking or smoking, has no limits. While there's money, there's a bet. Effectively, there was nothing left of Bill's estate for his stepson, John. It was a sad outcome for his next of kin.

However, investigators were still busy on the case and were awaiting the post-mortem and toxicological reports from the death.

Bill Adamson's body arrived at the Glebe Department of Forensic Medicine during the evening of 17 April 2010 and the post-mortem was carried out at 9 am on 20 April by Dr Isabella Brouwer. It was apparent that the body of the elderly man was 'in an early state of decomposition with extensive autolytic changes [breakdown of tissues] in the organs.' Other than that, it presented that of a well-nourished elderly male with no serious health issues.

However, the toxicological analysis of a post-mortem preserved blood sample was found to contain a morphine (free) level of 3.8 milligrams per litre and an alcohol level of 0.010 grams per 100 millilitres of blood. In addition, promethazine (Phenergan) was detected.

The morphine was the main subject of interest, and being well into the lethal range, it had clearly resulted in his death.

Bill was not known to drink alcohol and none had been brought to the motel, so the detection of a small amount of the substance in his blood was no doubt due to bacterial and/or yeast fermentation of the glucose in his blood, as his body was showing signs of decomposition. Also, the detection of promethazine was not unexpected, as some Phenergan medication had been found in his satchel of medication at the motel. It had been used to treat his skin allergies.

Promethazine also has potent anti-emetic and anti-nausea properties, which can prevent the nausea/emesis that can occur with high doses of morphine. Phenergan would have assisted the absorption of the morphine and prevented vomiting occurring, thus ejecting the poisonous dosage administered to Bill's body. No morphine medication was found in his personal possessions, but an almost empty foil pack of MS Contin (morphine sulphate) was found in Kerry's possession, although she had been prescribed them for her own pain. Senior Constable Anthony Holmes was keen to link the morphine tablets to her, and so I suggested comparing an isotopic profile of the morphine in the tablets to the morphine found in Bill's blood. However, that complicated procedure proved unnecessary, as the foil pack only had Kerry's fingerprints on it.

In any case, I concluded in my final report that the elevated blood concentration of morphine, along with the presence of promethazine, was more than sufficient to depress Mr William Adamson's respiratory system resulting in death.

With that evidence, it became a clear case of murder and Strike Force Human was formed to investigate. It began by monitoring Kerry Forrest's activities over the course of several months. In the meantime, she'd been busy moving around the state, eventually taking up a property under an assumed name. Shortly after she'd settled in her new accommodation, she was arrested and charged with murder. It was the evening of Valentine's Day, 14 February 2011. Life is full of ironies.

She appeared before Bega Local Court the following Tuesday, 22 February, where she was formally charged and refused bail. She also had a number of driving offences outstanding, including driving while disqualified, driving an unregistered and uninsured vehicle and displaying a misleading registration label. But those paled in comparison to the murder charge, which was adjourned to Campbelltown Local Court on 6 April. The driving offences, being less serious, were put over for a two-day committal hearing over 22 and 23 August 2012.

Given the very high level of free morphine (3.8 mg/L) detected in Bill Anderson's blood, I thought it prudent to have the total amount of morphine determined. That meant re-analysing the blood sample for bound morphine (the amount attached to the blood proteins) as well as the free morphine, or essentially, the total amount of morphine. The reason for doing that was that it would not only provide a way to establish how much of the drug had been inadvertently consumed by Bill Adamson prior to his death, but also present a means to determine approximately how long it had taken him to die from the effects of the drug by looking at the ratio of the free drug in relation to the total amount as a percentage.

The result came back at a whopping 11 milligrams per litre of morphine, which proved to be very useful evidence to be presented in court. With that information, I was able to give an estimate of the amount of drug consumed and an approximate length of time it had taken before Bill Adamson's respiratory system had shut down from the effects of the drug, thereby taking his life. In this case, it was 34.5 per cent, and the higher the ratio percentage, the shorter the time till death.

I was questioned at length about the pharmacological properties of morphine and the various ways that the drug can be taken into the human body. Then, predictably, I was asked about the amount of time it would have taken the deceased to die. I told the court that according to my calculations, 'death would have been in excess of three hours. If it was closer to 50 per cent, well, that indicates a much shorter period of time of death. So as you get the larger percentage the faster the person has passed away.'

Further questions were raised, including the number of 100-milligram MS Contin tablets Bill Adamson would have needed to consume to reach the morphine blood levels observed. I had earlier provided an estimate based on the free morphine figure. That proved to be very conservative, and I said to the court, 'I was relying mainly on the 3.8 milligrams of free morphine. Now, that was just an estimate and I said even this estimate may be conservative. Well, once I got the other analytical result of 11 per litre, and that's total morphine, it certainly indicated that my estimate was very conservative. So, based on that, I would indicate that it would have been greater than 10 tablets that had been consumed.'

Prior to my evidence, Dr Olaf Drummer from the Victorian Institute of Forensic Medicine had also given his expert opinion via an audio visual link to the court. It appeared we agreed on most of the issues, except for the number of MS Contin tablets consumed. His estimate of 'more than two tablets' was even more conservative than mine. Even though Bill Adamson had weighed only 64.5 kilograms at the time of his death, it had to be much more than two 100-milligram tablets! Nevertheless, after further police evidence was presented, the court found that sufficient evidence had been supplied to take the matter to the Supreme Court in Darlinghurst.

On 17 March 2014, the matter was subsequently heard before a judge-only trial, with Justice Peter Hidden presiding. Kerry Forrest, now 54, was brought into court in a wheelchair. She was wearing dark sunglasses and her head was bowed. It was a pathetic sight, and whether the scenario was for sympathy, or a genuine medical condition, only time was to tell. She waved briefly to her daughter, Kara, as she took her seat in the witness box.

Asked about the proceeds of the sale of the Kareela house, Kara told the court her mother had wanted to use the money to build a house in partnership with the elderly man, adding, 'We visited some display homes in Kellyville.'

She said not long after that, her mother had turned up at her Camden home, saying that Bill Adamson had died. 'She said that Bill had passed away and I asked if she had reported it. She said, no, she hadn't. She then went to the bathroom and splashed water on her face.'

She then related how Kerry Forrest had explained to her that she'd been out all day and that when she'd returned to the Maclin Motel where they were staying, she'd found him dead. It was then that she'd asked her and her boyfriend to call the police and ambulance, and to drop her around the corner of the motel.

Questioned about her mother's gambling problem, Ms Forrest said it was so bad that after Bill Adamson's death, she'd caught her playing two poker machines at once and had had to confiscate her debit cards.

Further evidence was provided by Detective Senior Constable Cate Fuller, who told the court that when she arrived at the motel room, she found Bill Adamson dead, and a case that had a large amount of medications in it. She also said that when she asked to search Kerry Forrest's bag, she became 'upset and defensive', and on searching the bag, she found Bill Adamson's wallet, along with his cash, health and credit cards.

The court also heard that Kerry Forrest had moved the proceeds of the sale of the Kareela property to her own bank accounts only days after Bill Adamson's death.

I was the last witness, and appeared on a fairly bleak, rainy day, which pretty much set the mood of the proceedings dealing with the death of an elderly war veteran. The questions put to me were very similar to those at the earlier Campbelltown Local Court hearing and so the answers were the same. However, the judge was curious as to how Kerry Forrest had managed to get Bill Adamson to ingest so much morphine that it resulted in his death. I don't like to speculate and prefer to deal with hard scientific facts, but I could understand where he was coming from, as it was a lot of one drug to consume, and a bitter one at that.

MS Contin is a sustained release dosage of morphine sulphate that is formulated to give patients relief from pain over an extended period of time. To get a rapid release and the high levels of morphine detected in Bill Adamson's blood, the tablets would have had to have been crushed up. But morphine, and indeed the opiates in general, are very bitter, so the taste needs to be disguised. I suggested that the drug powder could have been mixed into a beverage that was already bitter, such as coffee. But who knows, other than Kerry Forrest, whether the toxic dose of the powder was also mixed in other food she offered to Bill Adamson in his final hours.

In any case, the judge was satisfied that Kerry Forrest was guilty of the murder of William Adamson, having crushed up the tablets, possibly 10 or more, before feeding them to him, possibly in his coffee.

In his summing up, he said, 'Ms Forrest misappropriated Mr Adamson's money and killed him to prevent that misappropriation being exposed.'

It was a sad end for veteran who'd fought for Australia, only to be murdered decades later by a woman who posed as his carer.

On 27 November 2014 Justice Peter Hidden, after much deliberation, sentenced Kerry Forrest to a maximum of 25 years in jail, with a 19-year non-parole period. As she'd already spent nearly three years behind bars since her arrest in February 2011, she would be eligible for parole on 13 February 2030.

However, while in Long Bay prison, she was diagnosed with cervical cancer, along with several other serious medical conditions, which had left her in a wheelchair – hence the wheelchair in court.

Justice Hidden conceded that the minimum term was 'well beyond her life expectancy' of six to 18 months, given her medical conditions and that the cancer was considered incurable. However, he said it was not in his power to consider an early release. Only the state government and state parole authority could direct an early release in exceptional circumstances.

So Kerry Forrest was effectively given a life sentence for murdering an elderly man to support her gambling habit. Whether her cancer is truly incurable and her other medical problems treatable, only time will tell.

12.

THE ABERDEEN BUTCHER:
THE KATHERINE KNIGHT CASE

'All evils are equal when they are extreme.'
– Pierre Corneille, *Horace*

Katherine Knight.
PHOTOGRAPH COURTESY OF: *NY DAILY NEWS*

This story takes place in Aberdeen, a small township situated in the midst of the fertile pastoral and agricultural countryside of New South Wales. The town is located on the side of a hill, alongside the Hunter River, between Muswellbrook and Scone on the New England Highway. It was named after Aberdeen, in Scotland, and is 273 kilometres north of Sydney. The 2006 census recorded its population as 1791.

The district around Aberdeen was once occupied by the Wanaruah Aboriginal people. Because so few written records of Aboriginal Australia were kept, it's difficult to determine their lifestyle in pre-colonial Australia. However, it is known that the Wanaruah had trade and ceremonial links with another aboriginal tribe, the Kamilaroi, who may also have occupied the area. They were peaceful people who lived off the land, their favourite meal being goanna, along with kangaroo and assorted wildlife, which was roasted over campfire coals after being gutted and stuffed with grass. A traditional aboriginal feast for this area.

Many years later, the colonists moved in and established an abattoir to cater for the processing of fat beef cattle that were then raised on the rich pastures in the surrounding areas of the newly established township. That and the mining industry became the mainstays of Aberdeen. However, the abattoir was the main employer, providing work for more than 400 people from the town and surrounding areas, such as Scone.

It was in this setting, that one of the most gruesome murders in Australia's history took place.

■

Katherine Mary Knight was born about half an hour after her fraternal twin sister, Joy Gwendoline, at Tenterfield Hospital in north-western New South Wales on 24 October 1955. Their father, Ken, was a skilled slaughter man, working at the local abattoir. He and his wife, Barbara, now had eight children, six of whom were boys. It was a tough call supporting a family of that size, as Ken's wages had to stretch to feed 10 people, seven days a week.

Every meal had to count and Barbara's work was cut out with cooking, cleaning, sewing and raising the eight little ones. One night's lamb roast had to be turned into the following day's shepherd's pie, and so on, with other offerings for the rest of week. All in all, a typical working Australian family of those times.

Katherine was generally a pleasant girl, and her red hair and freckles earned her the nickname of 'the speckled hen'. Very much a loner, with only a couple of friends, she spent a lot of time playing with her dolls. However, she loved animals, or at least, pretty much any creature that was injured. Sadly, she wasn't allowed to have any pets because her father kept greyhounds and was afraid they would be eaten by the dogs, but, undeterred, she still picked up injured strays, small birds and so on, took them home and nursed them back to health.

Unfortunately, that good nature started to dissipate as she got older, when she also started to experience extraordinary rages over relatively minor upsets. She began to savour the smells of the meat industry and developed a yearning to work at the abattoir like her father. When she left Muswellbrook High School at the age of 15, supposedly almost illiterate, she landed a job as a cutter in a clothing factory. It wasn't exactly what she was looking for, and after a year, she left and got a position at the abattoir, cutting up offal. She loved it, and her enthusiasm was eventually rewarded when she was promoted to boning and presented with her own set of butcher knives, which she proudly hung over her bed so that they 'would always be handy if I needed them'. She was said to have been as raunchy and heartless as any male worker, and appeared to be quite proud of it. A tough woman in a tough environment.

In 1974, at the age of 18, she married 22-year-old co-worker, David Stanford Kellett, a former railway worker turned slicer. The couple arrived at the marriage service on Katherine's motorcycle, with a very drunk Kellett on the pillion seat. Katherine's mother took him aside and warned, 'You better watch this one or she'll fucking kill you. Stir her up the wrong way or do the wrong thing and you're fucked. Don't ever think of playing up on her, she'll fucking kill you.'

David just laughed it off, but Barbara wasn't joking, and it was said that Katherine tried to strangle him on their wedding night after he'd fallen asleep following several heavy bouts of sex.

Later on, David Kellett took another job at the abattoir, stunning pigs with a stun gun, which Katherine allegedly enjoyed watching.

Their first child, Melissa Ann, was born on 11 May 1976, but the marriage had now become very shaky, and David had begun an affair with another Aberdeen woman. Unable to handle Katherine's moods and rages, he took off to Queensland with his now pregnant mistress. That relationship was doomed and ended soon after the birth of the child.

Katherine was devastated by David's desertion and took her rage out on their newborn daughter, leaving the two-month-old baby in the middle of a railway track to be killed by the next train. Fortunately, Ted Abrahams, a pensioner who lived in a small room on the ground floor of the Aberdeen Hotel, heard the baby crying. He'd been foraging along the top of an embankment near the tracks at the time and rescued the child, just minutes before a train passed through!

Later that same day, Katherine grabbed an axe from a woodpile and started swinging it above her head and threatening people. She was apprehended by police and taken to St Elmo's Hospital in Tamworth for treatment, where she was subsequently discharged, with the doctors saying she was suffering from postnatal depression.

Soon after that, on Tuesday 3 August, Katherine slashed a young woman's face with a knife after the woman told her that Melissa was sick. She demanded that the poor woman take her to her husband. Having little option but to comply, the bleeding woman drove to the Bogas petrol station for petrol, but managed to escape. In the meantime, Katherine grabbed a little boy and threatened to slash him. When the police arrived, she was holding the child with one hand and a knife in the other. The two officers, choosing a less violent approach to defuse the situation, grabbed a couple of broomsticks and tried to knock the knife out of Katherine's hand, all the while telling her to drop the weapon. After prodding her several times with the broomsticks, she did and she was promptly arrested. The police then took her to a doctor in Muswellbrook, who issued a Schedule 2 under the Mental Health Act, and she was taken to Morisset Psychiatric Hospital for treatment, where she was diagnosed with personality disorder.

While she was in the hospital, her three-month-old baby daughter was looked after by her grandparents, Barbara and Ken. Katherine was subsequently discharged after six days into Jean Dobson's (David Keller's mother) care and custody, and soon after, Katherine, David and their baby daughter Melissa got back together, living in a rented bungalow in Woodridge, Queensland, where David drove trucks and Katherine took up a job boning carcasses at the Dinmore Abattoir in nearby Ipswich.

Despite the many difficulties experienced in the marriage, the couple did what warring spouses often do: they had another baby. Natasha Maree Kellett was born on 6 March 1980 in Nambour hospital.

Four years later, Katherine and David again separated. Katherine moved in with her parents in Aberdeen before renting a house in Muswellbrook and taking up work at her former place of employment, the Aberdeen abattoir. Her estranged husband moved to Alice Springs, where he found work as a trucker. Although they were separated, he was still a doting father, sending his girls presents and cards at Christmas and flowers on their birthdays. But they never knew about them because Katherine disposed of them before the girls were able to receive them. Both girls were crushed with disappointment.

In 1986, Katherine met a 38-year-old miner, David Saunders, at a local hotel. He was a good-natured hard drinker. Katherine turned on the charm and they soon hit it off. A few months later, he moved in with her and her two daughters.

But it wasn't long before the jealous rages began and she would throw him out of the house. He'd then move back to his apartment in Scone, and after a time, Katherine would go around and beg him to come back. He always returned. It appeared her voracious sexual appetite overrode any other concerns.

In May 1987, she slit the throat of his two-month-old dingo pup with one of her boning knives before going on to bash him on the head with a frying pan until he was unconscious. Those acts of violence were to show Saunders what would happen if he had an affair. And he hadn't even contemplated it!

In June 1988, Katherine gave birth to her third daughter. With a growing family, David Saunders decided to move out of their housing commission house and get one of their own. The house was paid off the following year when Katherine's worker's compensation (from a previous back injury received at the abattoir) came through. Meanwhile, Katherine had developed a macabre interest in dead animals and decorated their cottage with a variety of animal skins, cow and sheep skulls, water buffalo and steer horns, deer antlers, rusted animal traps, old-fashioned fur wraps and assorted stuffed animals and birds. It was a real museum of death.

Her rages hadn't stopped either. After yet another argument, she hit Saunders over the head with an iron and stabbed him with a pair of scissors. And in an act of real spite, she cut up all his clothes. Unsurprisingly, he left her, but when he returned later to see his daughter, he discovered that Katherine had taken out an Appended Violence Order (AVO). She'd told the police that he'd been abusing her and unfortunately they believed her. David Saunders then went away for good, not realising exactly how kind fate had been to him.

In 1990, Katherine met up with John 'Chillo' Chillingworth, a 43-year-old former abattoir co-worker, at the local hotel. At the time, he was unaware of her violent moods, but his friends warned him that she was bad news. Their relationship, while stormy, produced a son, Eric, who was born in 1991. But Katherine started having an affair with another Aberdeen local, John 'Pricey' Price, and the relationship with John Chillingworth ended after three years. Although he didn't know it at the time, he was very fortunate to be free of Katherine and was able to get on with his own life. However, the same could not be said of John Price. When he became entangled with Katherine, he was already the father of three children. Recently amicably separated from his wife, Colleen, he was feeling lonely and so quickly fell for Katherine's charms. It was 1993. They were both 38 and Pricey was totally smitten by her. He was a very popular man, very likeable and very generous. It was said that 'he would give you his last two bob'. A top bloke.

He worked at the Howick mines in Aberdeen, making a good living, and had a comfortable brick home in St Andrews Street, which had been left to him by his former wife. In 1995, Katherine moved in with him.

The house was quite luxurious compared to her 'dead animal museum' cottage and at first she treated him very well, as was her usual way, doing all the things that a loving wife does. Happy days. But it didn't last. The honeymoon period ended and the drinking and insane violence began.

In 1998, Katherine decided she wanted some permanence in their relationship and wanted John to marry her. He refused, and in retaliation, she videotaped some items allegedly stolen from work and sent the tape to his boss. The items were only outdated medical kits that had been given to him by the storeman but, nevertheless, it cost Pricey his job, a position he'd held and loved for 17 years. He was devastated.

He promptly threw Katherine out of his home and she returned to her dead animal museum in MacQueen Street. Pricey was now unemployed and lonely, and after a few months, they resumed their relationship, although she didn't move back into his house. Pricey's friends were amazed that he'd taken her back after what the 'poisonous speckled hen' (a disparaging term now given to Katherine) had done to him. Laurie Lewis, one of his close friends, said he wanted nothing more to do with 'that woman'. Unfortunately for Pricey, that had a knock-on effect, because other people would not associate with her, including his children, Rosemary, Jackeline (Jackie) and Johnathon, which led to him becoming isolated to some extent. Not only did the reconciliation come at considerable cost, but the emotional scars would never heal. Pricey could forgive, but he couldn't forget, and so the arguments and fights resumed.

Fortunately, he landed another job a few months after being sacked from Howick Mines. It was with a company called Bowditch and Partners Earthmoving Pty Ltd, and his bosses soon recognised his talents with heavy machinery.

However, Katherine was still consumed with her irrational and venomous need for revenge, and on 29 February 2000 she took a knife and stabbed him in the upper left chest, prompting him to take out an AVO against her to keep her away from him and his children. But so determined was she to up the ante, she just ignored it.

That same afternoon, Pricey said to his co-workers, somewhat prophetically, that if he didn't come into work the following day, it would be because Katherine had done him in. Concerned about the situation, his fellow co-workers said that he shouldn't go home, but Pricey felt that if he didn't, she would kill his children.

In the meantime, and unknown to him, Katherine had sent the children away for a sleepover at a friend's place, so when Pricey arrived home, there was no-one there. After an evening watching television, he took a shower and went to bed. Katherine sneaked into his house and woke him just after 11 pm. She must have used all her feminine wiles because they had sex, after which he fell asleep.

A night of terror was about to begin.

Katherine had brought her butcher's knife with her, and it was within easy reach. The first blow was struck without warning, followed by several others to his naked chest. She was now doing what she had threatened many times before – she was murdering him. In stark terror and agony, Pricey woke up and leapt out of bed, running down the hallway, with Katherine in relentless pursuit, all the time stabbing continuously at her mortally wounded victim. Blood from his numerous wounds stained the bedding, carpet and walls as he made a desperate attempt to escape. But the blade kept plunging into him. The pain was unbearable and his lungs were so badly damaged, he couldn't shout to raise the alarm. Amazingly, he clung to life, staggering to the front door and leaving a bloody hand print on the door frame. But he couldn't make it through and he was dragged back into the house where he collapsed. The stabbings continued and he slid down the wall of the entrance foyer, where he died. An autopsy was later to reveal that he'd been stabbed at least 37 times in both the front and back of his body, with many of the wounds damaging vital organs.

With Pricey dead, Katherine stripped off her bloodstained clothing and had a shower. Then she went into Aberdeen town and withdrew a sum of $500 from Pricey's account at the ATM at 2.32 am followed by a further sum of $500 at 2.35 am – a total of $1000 (the maximum allowed at one drawing).

But her grisly night's work and revenge were still not complete.

At 6 am, a neighbour noticed that Pricey's white Ford Mondeo sedan was still in the driveway. That's so unlike Pricey, he thought. Normally, he'd have been away to work and he was known as being very punctual, so when he didn't arrive at Bowditch and Partners, his employer sent a fellow worker around to his house to see if he was okay. The neighbour and worker noticed Pricey's work boots were still lined up at the front door, as was his custom. Thinking that he may have overslept, they tried waking him by knocking on his bedroom window. It was then that they spotted blood stains on the front door and contacted the police.

Sergeant Furlonger and Senior Constables Maude and Matthews arrived at the St Andrews Street property 25 minutes later, at 8.10 am. They tried the front and back doors, finding each to be locked, and used a crowbar to gain entry via the laundry door. The police officers had decades of experience between them, but nothing could have prepared them for what they were about to witness.

Led by Sergeant Furlonger, they entered the premises with their weapons drawn. There was blood everywhere and a large pool of blood near the entrance foyer. Then what was thought to be a blanket hanging in a doorway arch leading into the lounge turned out to be, on closer inspection, John Price's exterior layer of skin hanging from a meat hook.

'Oh my God, she's skinned him!' one of the officers gasped.

It was a human pelt, expertly removed in one piece.

Moving further into the house, they found the victim's decapitated remains on the lounge-room floor, near a small foyer leading to the front door. The body was raw and bloodless. Given the injuries and blood loss, that was hardly surprising. The left arm of John Price's body was draped over an empty 1.25 litre soft drink bottle and his legs were crossed. A butcher's knife was found close by. (Two more knives were later found in the kitchen.)

As the police officers moved through the house, they caught the smell of something that had been cooking coming from the kitchen. Further extreme horrors were to be revealed.

There was a large pot, still warm, on the stove. On opening the lid, they saw John Price's skinned head, along with a quantity of vegetables. After Katherine had decapitated him, she'd cooked parts of his body, serving up the meat with a variety of vegetables, including baked potatoes and gravy, in three settings at the dinner table. She'd also prepared notes alongside the plates, each one having the name of one of his children written on it.

Many of the surfaces were heavily bloodstained. A third piece of cooked meat (later identified to be from John Price's left buttock) was found in the backyard. (It has been speculated that Katherine Knight had attempted to eat it but had been unable to do so and tossed it onto the back lawn. However, that has never been established to any degree of certainty.)

A further bloodstained note was found on a small display cabinet in the lounge room, near the hanging skin. It read, 'Now play with little Johns dick John Price. Time got back Johnathon for rapping [raping] my douter [daughter]. You to Ross and Little John.'

The words were found to be nonsense.

The police officers then checked the bathroom and found it was empty, save for a black nightie tossed carelessly over the side of the bath. It was heavily bloodstained with what appeared to be flecks of meat adhering to the fabric.

Then they heard a loud snoring sound coming from the main bedroom and looked through the door. The light switch was bloodstained and the sleeping body of Katherine Knight was lying fully clothed on the double bed. With some difficulty, she was roused and handcuffed. At 8.25 am, an ambulance was summoned, along with police backup, and the house and surrounding area were declared to be a crime scene.

Katherine Knight was sitting on the ground behind a police vehicle when the ambulance arrived. She was dishevelled, her face was flushed and her speech was slurred. Upon examination, the ambulance crew formed the opinion that she'd taken an excessive amount of medication. (Empty packets of medication were later found on the kitchen bench of the house.) She was loaded into the ambulance, which left at 9.16 am, and was placed under the care of medical staff. A blood sample was taken as standard procedure.

The subsequent toxicology report revealed that the blood sample contained fluvoxamine 0.22 milligrams per litre and promethazine 0.21 milligrams per litre. No alcohol was detected.

Fluvoxamine is a serotonin re-uptake inhibitor (SNRI) antidepressant that can result in dizziness and drowsiness. It's available under the trade name Luvox, which is used to treat emotional depression. The therapeutic range for this drug is 0.05 to 0.25 milligrams per litre of blood, meaning the level found in Katherine Knight's blood was towards the top end.

Promethazine is a phenothiazine-type antihistamine that can also result in dizziness and drowsiness, and would therefore exacerbate the effects of fluvoxamine. It's available under several trade names, including Phenergan, which is used to treat hayfever and allergy symptoms. The therapeutic range for this drug is 0.1 to 0.4 milligrams per litre of blood, so the level found in Katherine Knight's blood was mid-range.

Neither of the drugs were in the toxic range, but the two together resulted in Knight being found in a deep sleep. The outcome could have been quite different if she'd also consumed an appreciable quantity of alcohol in addition to the medication, but as it was, she was able to sleep it off and was not in any danger.

I found from earlier research that in most drug overdoses involving promethazine only, the levels were either very high (greater than 2 milligrams per litre − 10 times more than that found in Katherine's blood), or another central nervous system depressant, such as oxazepam (Serepax) or alcohol, was present, and sometimes both.

Detective Sergeant Bob Wells and Detective Senior Constable Peter Muscio from the Maitland crime scene team were tasked with further investigations into John Price's gruesome murder, and on 6 March 2000, after the alleged suicide attempt, Katherine Knight was formally charged with the murder, at Maitland District Hospital. She'd been placed in the psychiatric ward, where psychiatrists had assessed her mental state, concluding that she'd been sane when committing her heinous crimes.

Katherine Knight's defence counsel initially applied for the charge of guilty to be reduced to one of manslaughter. Not unsurprisingly, it was rejected and Katherine was arraigned to appear before the court on 2 February 2001. She entered a plea of not guilty. The trial was initially set for 23 July, but was postponed due to the illness of her counsel and given a new date of 15 October.

When the trial began, Justice Barry O'Keefe (jokingly known as the

Mild One, as he was the brother of rocker, Johnny O'Keefe, the Wild One) offered the 60 jury prospects the option of being excused from duty due to the graphic nature of the evidence. Five accepted. Several more declined after the witness list had been read out.

The defence attorneys for Katherine Knight then spoke to the judge, who adjourned proceedings until the following day. When the trial commenced the next morning, Katherine Knight surprisingly pleaded guilty, and so the jury was dismissed. The plea saved John Price's family and a number of witnesses the ordeal of going through a lengthy traumatic trial.

In spite of that and the fact that Katherine's legal team had planned to defend her by claiming amnesia and dissociation, Justice O'Keefe ordered a psychiatric assessment to establish whether Katherine Knight understood the consequences of a guilty plea and whether she was fit to make such a plea. Although admitting her guilt, Katherine still refused to take responsibility for her very savage actions, and she was held in custody.

Several forensic psychiatrists, including Dr Robert Delaforce, determined that she'd been totally sane when she'd committed the crimes. He concluded, 'What she did on the night was part of her personality, her nature, herself, but it is not a feature of borderline personality disorder, it is not even significantly connected.'

On Thursday 8 November 2001, 618 days after the murder of John Price, his family returned to court, hoping that justice would prevail at the sentencing. Justice O'Keefe had much to consider. There was no doubt that the barbaric murder fell into the worst case category, and under section 23A of the *Crimes Act 1900*, he had a choice of either sending Katherine to prison for the term of her natural life or he could grant her mercy and impose a long fixed sentence.

He began to read from his lengthy judgment, reiterating what had occurred on or about 29 February 2000. He described the manner in which John Price had died, which proved to be very hard for his children, who broke down, with one daughter having to leave the courtroom to compose herself. Then he moved on to Katherine's attempted suicide, saying it hadn't appeared genuine, quoting as evidence the relevant bits from the toxicology report that showed the blood levels of the drugs detected had been within therapeutic limits. He also noted that Katherine would have required a steady hand and much skill to remove the skin from John Price's deceased body in one piece, which included his head, face, nose, neck, torso, genitals and legs.

As for mercy, Justice O'Keefe said, 'The prisoner, Katherine Mary Knight, does not qualify for mercy. She engaged in cruel, vicious behaviour to Mr Price. She showed him no mercy. She has not expressed any contrition or remorse. If released, she poses a serious threat to the security of society. I'm satisfied beyond any doubt that such a murder was premeditated. I'm further satisfied in the same way that not only did she plan the murder, but she also enjoyed the horrific acts which followed in its wake as part of a ritual of dead and defilement.'

His Honour continued, 'The things which she did after the death of Mr Price indicate cognition, volition, calm and skill. I am satisfied beyond reasonable doubt that her evil actions were playing out of her resentments arising out of her rejection by Mr Price, her impending expulsion from Mr Price's home, which he wanted to retain for his children.'

Further, 'As I have said, the prisoner showed no mercy whatsoever to Mr Price. The last minutes of his life must have been a time of abject terror for him, as they were a time of utter enjoyment for her. At no time did the prisoner express any regret for what she had done or any remorse for having done it; not even through the surrogacy of counsel. Her attitude in that regard is consistent with her general approach to the many acts of violence which she has engaged in against her various partners.'

Justice O'Keefe addressed the court for over an hour and said in his concluding comments, 'The only appropriate penalty for the prisoner is life imprisonment and that parole should never be considered for her.'

He then looked up from his judgment and asked Katherine Knight to stand before delivering the judgment that John Price's family were anxious to hear.

'Katherine Mary Knight, you have pleaded guilty to, and been convicted of, the murder of John Charles Thomas Price at Aberdeen in the State of New South Wales, on or about 29th February, 2000. In respect of that crime, I sentence you to imprisonment for life.'

She was led her away to the cells below the courtroom to await her final transport to Mulawa Women's Correctional Centre, where she would begin the rest of her life in prison. She made history by becoming the first woman in Australia to be jailed for the term of her natural life.

Someone once said that the way to measure a man and how he led his life was at his funeral. I'm not so sure about that, given the lavish funerals that well-known gangsters have had at their deaths. But in John Price's case, I have to agree. He was a decent, hardworking Australian who loved his women, his kids, his mates and his beer, and pretty much in that order!

Pricey was truly a rough diamond, and it was standing room only at St Alban's Anglican Church, Muswellbrook on 10 March 2000. Many others were unable to get a place in the church, and had to listen to the service outside.

When Pricey was alive, he was known as a top bloke, and it showed at his funeral, with the hundreds of people who came to pay their respects. His best friend, Laurie Lewis, and his two previous bosses, Geoffrey Bowditch and Peter Cairnes delivered moving eulogies before the congregation. After the church service, the funeral cortege made its way along the New England Highway to the Aberdeen cemetery, where he was finally laid to rest.

In June 2006, Katherine Knight appealed her life sentence, claiming that the mutilation of John Price's body after his death was not relevant to the seriousness of the offence and that she hadn't received an adequate discount for her guilty plea. However, in September, justices Peter McClellan, Michael Adams and Megan Latham dismissed the appeal in the New South Wales Court of Criminal Appeal.

Justice Adams said the mutilation of the body was closely associated with the murder such that 'it must be regarded as an integral part of the killing itself. It demonstrates the extraordinary extent of the applicant's brutality.'

Justice McClellan commented, 'This was a violent and cruel crime during which the deceased must have suffered extreme trauma. The crime was the product of a violent personality intent upon claiming the life of her de facto in a relationship which was plainly failing. The psychiatric evidence indicates that her personality is unlikely to change in the future, and if released, she would be likely to inflict serious injury, perhaps death, on others. The deceased's family may be at particular risk. This was an appalling crime, almost beyond contemplation in a civilised society.'

Katherine Knight's papers were marked, 'Never to be released'.

At the Mulawa Women's Correctional Centre (now known as Silverwater Women's Correctional Centre), she initially worked as a cleaner in the governor's office, but now works in a head-phone factory.

It has been 19 years since she was taken into custody. The now white-haired 63-year-old woman with a benign smile and twinkling eyes behind owlish glasses, has apparently found religion, paints, knits, makes pottery and is known as 'The Nanna' by other inmates.

However, prison officers never take their eyes off her and it is said that she can't have a cellmate in case she kills again. And, despite her alleged culinary skills, she is not, unsurprisingly, allowed near knives.

13.

PSYCHOSIS AND A CASE OF PATRICIDE: SHAMIN FERNANDO

'Schizophrenia cannot be understood without understanding despair.'
– R. D. Laing

This was a most unusual case. Most of the cases I've dealt with over the years have involved offences that have occurred while under the influence of various drugs, whether legal, for example, alcohol, or illegal, for example, methylamphetamine. Here, the perpetrator was suffering from a lengthy mental illness, which was controlled by several medications. However, because the medications appeared to have either been taken in insufficient amounts, or worse, not to have been taken at all, psychosis took over with deadly effects, and so the tragedy occurred.

■

Shamin Fernando was born on 16 July 1967 in Sri Lanka, and migrated to Australia with her family four years later. She had two sisters, Dayanthi and Michelle, and enjoyed a normal childhood. When she reached her early twenties, she unfortunately began to suffer from schizophrenia and a major depressive disorder. Not too surprisingly, those medical conditions impacted upon her working life, wellbeing and personal relationships. Nevertheless, with medical care and appropriate medications, clozapine (Clozaril) and venlafaxine (Efexor – XR), she was able to maintain a normal life, even completing a degree in communications at the University of Technology, Sydney, and landing a job managing a community radio station associated with Macquarie University.

However, she started to become reluctant to take the medication, in particular, clozapine, saying to her mother, 'If I accept that I have got this illness, I'll never be able to trust my own judgment again.'

But due to her mental health, she had a strained relationship with her father, Vincent 'Lalin' Fernando, even with the medication. To further complicate matters, she began to self-medicate and became a heavy user of cannabis. Excessive cannabis use is known to exacerbate an underlying psychotic conditions.

She became somewhat delusional, thinking there was a global conspiracy against her, organised initially by a former university lecturer and later by her father. Worse still, she believed she was under surveillance and that her personal information was being broadcast while the details were being withheld from her.

As for her father, he was very loving towards all his children and was eager to seek a reunion with Shamin. But mental illness doesn't reason in the usual way, and she perceived her father as a serious threat.

In preparation for dealing with the 'conspiracy', she joined the Sydney Pistol Club at La Perouse, a suburb in south-eastern Sydney, after filling out an application form and providing two character references. No mention was made of her mental illness, and she checked the section referring to that condition as 'no'. She now had access to a firearm and plenty of ammunition.

At 9 am on Sunday 22 August 2010, Shamin went to the Sydney Pistol Club in order to carry out some target practice on the range. She signed out a club-owned .22 calibre Ruger semiautomatic pistol and bought two boxes of ammunition, each containing a hundred rounds, from the club's duty officer, George Petas, a firearms dealer. She then joined in the 'match of the day' and fired off 70 rounds of ammunition during the session. After the session finished, she hid the weapon in her handbag, along with remainder of the ammunition, before leaving the firing range.

At 1.45 pm the same day, Shamin returned to her one-bedroom unit at 12/2 Victoria Road, Glebe and loaded six bullets into the magazine of the Ruger pistol, which she placed under a quilt on the bed. Then she called her father on both his mobile phone and home landline, leaving messages for him to call her. 'Dad, I need help to load some software now, please ring me back.'

At 2.19 pm, she eventually contacted him and repeated her request. Thinking it could be the beginning of a reconciliation, her father was eager to assist. 'Yes, of course, what time?'

'Oh, about three will be fine.'

Meanwhile, the pistol club's gun-keeper, Patrick Slavik, had noticed that the gun signed out to her hadn't been signed back in according to the club's regulations, but he thought it was a clerical error and that the gun had been returned, only realising it hadn't been when he went to put the guns from the day's activities into a locker. Now worried, he phoned the club captain, who called the secretary to check Shamin's details in the gun register. The secretary then tried unsuccessfully to call her at 2.42 am.

Shamin's father arrived promptly on the hour at the Glebe unit and was ushered into the lounge room, where the computer was sitting on a desk. He pulled up a chair and commenced work, loading disks into the system. While her father was busy, Shamin went to her bedroom and pulled the loaded Ruger out from under the quilt. She then opened the bedroom door and moved into the lounge, where she aimed the pistol at the back of her father's head and fired off five rounds. The first shot misfired, but the other four hit him. He stood up and cried out in pain before staggering towards the kitchen, where he collapsed. Not sure whether he was dead or not, Shamin went back to the bedroom and loaded more rounds into the pistol, returning to the lounge and firing a further three rounds into his twitching body. The execution was now complete.

Shamin then sat down and contemplated the situation for a while, wondering if the neighbours had heard and if they would call round. But nothing happened, so at 3.14 pm, she called 000 and asked for the police, saying she'd just shot her father in the back of his head and he was now dead. Just two minutes earlier, the pistol club captain had called police to tell them that she'd stolen a gun from the club.

The police arrived shortly after and the first police officer on the scene, after establishing they were at the right address and that he was talking to Shamin, shouted through the door, 'Just step out of the flat with your hands up and walk out backwards.'

Realising the situation she was now in, Shamin yelled, 'I'm walking out backwards now and my hands are up in the air.'

As she emerged, a further instruction was barked, 'Get on your knees!'

Shamin duly dropped to the floor and was asked where the gun was.

'On the sideboard.'

But the police, not knowing the situation fully, weren't taking any risks, so they handcuffed her and she was taken down to police headquarters.

In the meantime, an ambulance arrived with paramedics, and after assessing that Vincent Fernando was dead, took his body to the Glebe mortuary, not far from where his delusional daughter lived.

As with most police investigations, and particularly serious offences, a strike force was initiated. This one was called Strike Force Simmie.

At about 6.30 pm that day, Shamin was interviewed via ERISP (Electronically Recorded Interview of a Suspected Person) at the police station in Newtown.

An ERISP is a police procedure where a person being interviewed is recorded both on audio and video. The general legal advice in such a situation is that they only give their name, address and date of birth, but should not answer any further questions until a criminal lawyer is contacted. A document entitled Caution and Summary of Part 9 of the *Law Enforcement (Powers and Responsibilities) Act 2002* is read to the interviewee prior to the session.

On legal advice, Shamin initially decided not to say anything. However, after being asked if she was happy to be interviewed about the shooting, she answered in the affirmative. The usual procedural questions were then asked before the interview moved on to the events of the afternoon.

'What was the purpose of him [Vincent Fernando] coming around? When you made the phone call, what were you thinking?'

'I wanted to shoot him.'

'So why did you ask him to come round and load software on your computer?'

'If I asked him to come round so I could shoot him, I don't think he'd come.'

Then, chillingly, she chuckled at the thought.

Further questioning dealt with how she managed to remove the gun from the pistol club undetected, how and when the gun was loaded and where the gun had been stored prior to the killing.

Asked why she'd joined the pistol club, she replied without hesitation, that she'd wanted to get a firearm to 'shoot the old man' (referring to her father).

Finally, the questioning came down to the motive for the killing.

'Why did you want to shoot your father?'

It was here, under further questioning, that it became evident that Shamin was quite delusional. She said that she was trapped in a reality-style TV show and that her father was the main producer. It involved being monitored by hidden cameras and the show was broadcast on the internet and television. It also required her to pretend that it wasn't happening and that her thoughts were actually psychotic delusions, meaning she had to take medications, see doctors and not to discuss the show or the production. Essentially, she felt trapped in this Truman-like show that was supposedly orchestrated by her father, and she thought the only way to get out of it was by killing him. 'Yeah, shooting the old man was the only way out.'

Someone once said, 'There is no reality, only perception,' and in this case, a loving father was unfortunately perceived as a manipulating television producer trapping his daughter into a pseudo reality-style TV show. Further from reality, it would be hard to get.

Given the seriousness of the offence, the matter went before the NSW Supreme Court and Justice Peter Hall on 15 December 2011. The court was told that members of the Sydney Pistol Club rang police at 3.12 pm on 22nd August 2010 to report the missing Ruger gun, just two minutes before Shamin Fernando rang police to confess to having shot her father. The court also heard that Shamin lured her father to her Glebe unit on the pretext of getting him to load software onto her computer. However, the main issue raised was how a probationary gun club member had been able to take a weapon away from the pistol club so easily.

A further issue raised was that of mental illness, as Shamin had crossed 'no' by the question on the club form that asked whether she had any mental illness preventing her from using a firearm safely, and there had been no checking of the information she'd provided.

My evidence was rather brief. I said, 'I am of the opinion that at the time of the incident, given the symptoms described of Ms Shamin Fernando, they would appear to be consistent with her untreated medical condition said to be paranoid schizophrenia. However, it appears a blood sample was not taken at the time, so it is not possible [for me] to determine whether she was adequately treated for her medical conditions or not.'

But the previous evidence given by other witnesses indicated that Shamin's mental illness had not been adequately treated.

After considering the evidence, Justice Hall found that because of her mental illness, 44-year-old Shamin Fernando was not guilty of murdering her 70-year-old father. However, she was remanded in custody under section 38 of the Mental Health Act until such time that psychiatrists determine she is fit to be released. Until then, she will receive treatment at the forensic hospital at Long Bay.

Shamin's mother, Carmen, while grieving over the incident, said that her daughter was not a criminal. 'She's a victim, just as we are. This happened because she was inadequately treated and because of the access she was given to a firearm despite being seriously mentally ill.'

Following the shooting, the NSW commissioner of police, Mr Andrew Scipione, tried to suspend all shooting activities at the Sydney Pistol Club, but was prevented from doing so by an Administrative Decisions Tribunal, which said the club had tightened its regulations and that closure of the facility would adversely affect its 150 members and put the club's survival at risk.

However, the instructors at the pistol club failed in their duty of care. Subsequently, George Petas and Patrick Slavik were prosecuted. Petas was found guilty of selling ammunition to an unlicensed shooter, although no conviction was recorded, while Slavik was found guilty of failing to supervise Shamin Fernando and failing to keep a firearm in a safe place. He was fined for both offences.

Since the tragedy, Shamin's sister, Michelle, a criminal lawyer, has been on a campaign to tighten a loophole in the gun laws. She believes that a weakening of the NSW firearms laws in 2008 was partly responsible for her father's death. She cannot understand how her mentally ill sister managed to walk out of the Sydney Pistol Club with a semiautomatic handgun along with an estimated 130 rounds of ammunition in her handbag.

After the Port Arthur massacre, where 35 people were murdered, the then prime minister, John Howard, brought in laws to ensure that anyone possessing and shooting a gun had to be licensed. Unfortunately, the Shooters Party brought in an amendment (6B) to the NSW Firearms Act in 2008, which was supported by the Labor government under Bob Carr at the time, which allowed people aged 12 years and older to enter a gun club and shoot without a licence. Furthermore, shooters were no longer required to wait 28 days to permit a police background check for a criminal record, domestic violence or mental illness.

A spokesperson from the police minister's office said, 'Labor, under Bob Carr, made several changes to gun laws that were a betrayal of the Howard government's National Firearms Agreement.'

Asked whether the minister was comfortable with 12-year-olds shooting at gun clubs, he replied, 'We are comfortable with the resources of the NSW police force deployed through the NSW Firearms Registry to ensure that shooting is carried out safely and under supervision.'

In true politician-speak, he effectively ducked the question.

Despite the shooting and killing of Vincent Fernando and a change in government, the 2008 change to the Firearms Act unfortunately still stands.

14.

DEATH HOUSE LANDLADY: DOROTHEA PUENTE

'Dorothea Puente rented out rooms to the elderly (at their peril)'
– Jodi Picoult

Dorothea Helen Puente.
COURTESY OF *THE SACRAMENTO BEE.*

Dorothea Puente was born in Redlands, California, on 9 January 1929 as Dorothea Helen Gray to parents Trudy Mae and Jesse James Gray. She had a tough upbringing, as both of her parents were alcoholics. In addition, her mother was a sex worker and her father had suicidal tendencies. In 1937, she endured a double tragedy when only eight years old when her father died of tuberculosis and the following year her mother died in a car accident. With nowhere else to go, she was sent to an orphanage, where it is alleged she was sexually abused.

It was a very poor start in life and no doubt, adversely affected her views on life.

In the late 1980s the by then deceptively sweet little-old-lady, murdered at least nine people and buried seven of them in the backyard of her Victorian boarding house in 1426 F Street, Sacramento, California, producing a 'wiffy' backyard.

The house became a Sacramento symbol of horror.

■

Sacramento city is the capital of California and is situated in the Sacramento Valley along the Sacramento River at its junction with the American River 145 kilometres (90 miles) north-east of San Francisco and 72 kilometres (45 miles) north of Stockton.

Sacramento experiences long, hot, dry summers and cool, damp winters with periodic foggy spells, very similar to those experienced in San Francisco. Overall, it is a very pleasant place to settle down and enjoy the Californian lifestyle without the expensive price tag. It was hardly the place where one would expect a serial murderer to operate. Much less, the hardened criminal in the guise of an elderly sweet lady who 'took care' of Sacramento's impoverished people.

However, before Dorothea Puente (nee Gray) began her descent into a career of murder, she had a somewhat turbulent life. At the tender age of 16 she married a soldier by the name of Fred McFaul in 1945, who had returned from fighting in the Pacific during World War II. The couple had two daughters between 1946 and 1948. Clearly, she didn't want children as she sent one to live with relatives in Sacramento and the other child was placed in adoption. She became pregnant again but lost the child through a miscarriage. This was enough for McFaul, who left her in 1948.

Ever the enterprising woman, she set about forging checks to make ends meet. She was caught, jailed but was paroled after six months. Later, a chance meeting with a man she hardly knew resulted in another pregnancy. After giving birth to another daughter, this child was also given up for adoption.

Then in 1952, she met a Swedish man, Axel Johanson, and they endured a difficult 14-year marriage. During this time Dorothea extended her criminal career into prostitution while owning and managing a brothel, also working as a nurse's aide, caring for disabled and elderly people – and forging checks. In 1966, she divorced Johanson.

Shortly after, she met and married Roberto Puente, a man 19 years younger than her, in Mexico City. The marriage ended after two years. However, she still retained her married name, Puente. No children had resulted from either of these unions.

In about 1968, Dorothea Puente took over a three-storey, 16-bedroom care home in Sacramento, where she would then rent the upstairs apartment at 1426 F Street. But before launching into her murderous – and profitable – enterprise, Puente met and married Pedro Montalvo in 1976. He was a poor choice of partner who turned out to be a violent alcoholic, and the marriage, not too surprisingly, only lasted a few months.

It was only a distraction. A more lucrative business was afoot, cashing cheques from older people (men mostly) who were receiving benefits, forging their signatures and stealing their money. She was soon caught and subsequently charged with 34 counts of treasury fraud. Amazingly, she escaped a prison sentence and was placed on probation.

Now a hardened criminal in the body of elderly 'sweetness', Dorothea Puente changed her focus, and started renting out space in the home for Sacramento's indigent. In April 1982, Ruth Monroe (61 years), her friend and rental partner, who was living with Puente in her upstairs apartment, was found dead in her bed. The cause of death was found to be from a drug overdose from a combination of codeine and paracetamol (acetaminophen). (The latter is available under several trade names including Tylenol). Puente told police that Monroe was depressed because of her terminally ill husband. She was believed and the death was ruled as a suicide, despite the absence of a suicide note and reasonable cause.

Puente eventually inherited $6000 from Ruth Monroe's estate. This proved to be a jackpot but it wasn't all smooth sailing, as a 74-year-old pensioner, Malcolm McKenzie, accused Puente of drugging and stealing from him. (He was one of four other elderly people who Puente was eventually accused of drugging.) Police attended, Puente was arrested and subsequently convicted on 18 August 1982 of three charges of theft and sentenced to five years jail. During her interment, she began corresponding with Everson Gillmouth, a 77-year-old retiree living in Oregon, and they developed a penpal relationship. She was released in 1985, after serving only three years of her sentence and Everson was there, waiting to take her home in his red 1980 Ford pickup. What happened to Everson after this generous gesture, is anyone's guess. But it wasn't good.

In November 1985, a local handyman and carpenter, Ismael Florez, was hired by Puente to install some wood panelling and to construct a large box to store 'books and other items'. For his efforts he was paid for his labour plus an additional $800. In addition, he was given a red 1980 Ford pickup in good condition, as it belonged to her boyfriend in Los Angeles 'who no longer needed it'. Florez was then asked to transport the prepared, filled and now nailed shut box to a storage depot believing the contents were 'just junk'.

Puente accompanied him in the pickup with the grisly cargo while travelling along the Garden Highway in Sutter County and told Florez to stop the truck and leave the box at an unofficial household dumping site on the bank of the Feather River.

There the box stayed until 1 January 1986, when a fisherman saw the box floating about a metre from the river bank. Suspicious, he called the police. On opening the box, a badly decomposed body of an elderly man was found inside. It would be three years later before the body was finally identified as that of Everson Gillmouth.

In the meantime, Dorothea Puente collected Everson Gillmouth's pension cheques and to avert suspicions from his family, wrote letters explaining he had health issues and was unable to visit them.

Puente's 'room and board' business prospered, taking in 40 new tenants consisting mainly of elderly residents. She was popular with the local social workers because difficult and tough cases, including drug addicts and abusive tenants, were accepted. She routinely collected her tenants' mail before they saw it, cashing their cheques on their behalf and leaving them a small stipend, keeping the rest for herself for various 'expenses and luxuries'.

As Dorothea Puente had spent some time in jail for various offences, which included forging cheques, it wasn't surprising that parole officers came and visited her premises on a number of occasions, where she had been ordered previously to refrain from handling government cheques and to keep away from the elderly. But amazingly, despite the visits, no violations were ever recorded.

So, business went on as usual at 1426 F Street. Then more people started disappearing.

Neighbourhood suspicions were first aroused when a homeless alcoholic known simply as 'Chief' was engaged by Ms Puente to carry out a number of handyman duties, which entailed digging in the basement of the house, carting soil and rubbish away in a wheelbarrow and various other domestic duties. Chief disappeared shortly afterwards and a fresh concrete slab appeared in the garage where he had been previously working.

Worse, there were odd nauseating smells starting to come from the backyard. Naturally enough, the neighbours complained about the awful smells coming from Dorothea Puente's yard and she told them that she was having problems with the sewage backup and dead rats. The 'sweet old lady's' explanation seemed to appease them for a time, but still necessitated the closure of their windows and they didn't seem to mind her spreading quicklime around her yard to supress the smell.

On 11 November 1988 one of Ms Puente's tenants, Mr Alberto Montoya, a developmentally disabled man with schizophrenia, went missing. His social and case worker filed a missing person report which was passed onto police investigators. A search warrant was issued and police officers paid Dorothea Puente a call. After a few routine inquiries, police then turned their attention to the backyard of the apartment building and noticed disturbed soil in the yard.

Acting on an educated hunch, the area was excavated revealing well decomposed and decomposing bodies, some were mummified in bed sheets, duct tape and cloth. Law enforcement officers had found Alberto Montoya's body buried along with six other bodies.

Curiously, Dorothea Puente was not immediately a suspect following the initial investigation, and she was allowed to leave the premises, supposedly to buy a cup of coffee at a nearby cafe. Realising the jig was up she had packed a bag and fled to Los Angeles, where she met an elderly pensioner at a bar, introducing herself as Donna, and no doubt going through a well-rehearsed routine to befriend him. In the meantime, police had unearthed further bodies and these findings were aired through the media. Fortunately, the pensioner recognised her from the news footage on television and notified the authorities.

The FBI were called into the case and a nationwide manhunt took place. She was later found at a hotel in LA where she had adopted the name of Dorothea Johnson. As she was being escorted to the police car to be taken back to Sacramento to stand trial, she was heard to say, 'I used to be a very good person, at one time.' Silver-haired, wearing large round glasses and a smart red coat, the 59-year-old appeared like a kindly grandmother! Appearances can certainly deceive.

Dorothea Puente was subsequently charged with a total of nine murders. Firstly, her friend and rental partner Ruth Monroe (61); her boyfriend, Everson Gillmouth (77); and seven others who resided at the apartment house: Leona Carpenter (78); Alvaro 'Alberto' Montoya (51); Dorothy Miller (64); Benjamin Fink (55); James Gallop (62); Vera Faye Martin (64) and Betty Palmer (78). Their deaths were caused by medication overdoses and/or suffocation.

The last victim proved to be a puzzle as, unlike the others, the body had been mutilated and the head, hands and legs had been removed. Fortunately, a forensic investigator finally identified the remains as those of Betty Palmer, one of the boarders of the death house. Sadly, Ms Palmer's missing body parts were never found, despite intensive searches of the house and yard carried out by police investigators.

Dorothea Puente's trial was transferred to Monterey County, California, on application by her defence lawyers, Kevin Clymo and Peter Vlautin. The prosecutor, was John O'Mara, a homicide supervisor in Sacramento County District Attorney's office.

After a number of legal hurdles, the trial began in October 1992, four years after her arrest. John O'Mara called 130 witnesses to testify against Puente and explained to the jury how she had used sleeping tablets (such as flurazepam, Dalmane) to drug her tenants and then suffocate them with pillows while they were unconscious. Their dismembered bodies were then buried in the backyard. In the meantime, she was collecting an estimated $5000 a month from cashing their social security cheques.

Dorothea Puente's defence lawyer, Kevin Clymo, introduced her long-lost daughter, and described her mother's sad upbringing. He said, in an effort to draw sympathy from the jury, that she took in tenants that no-one else wanted,.

The jury found it difficult to believe that the matronly grandmother was capable of carrying out such heinous crimes. However, after deliberating for over a month, Puente was found guilty of only three murders. The jury were unable to agree on the other six.

In the end, Dorothea Puente was convicted for three of the murders and received two life sentences without parole. She was imprisoned at the Central California Women's Facility (CCWF) in Chowchilla, California. There she maintained for the rest of her life that she was innocent and that all of her tenants had died of 'natural causes'.

But one wonders, if this was so, why dismember them and bury them in the garden? Why not a simple 911 call, followed by an ambulance, where paramedics would have taken the bodies off the premises and treated any illnesses the patients suffered. Clearly other issues were afoot, mostly sinister.

On 27 March 2011 Dorothea Puente died in her prison cell at Chowchilla Prison at the age of 82, from natural causes – a number of years more than her poor victims had.

Well, there the story appeared to have ended. But the house at 1426 F Street with its horrible background has held a rather macabre fascination for many people. In 2011, a couple, Barbara Holmes and her husband

Tom Williams purchased the house at a public auction for $US215,000 knowing the house's history.

As Tom Williams explained, they wanted to play with the ghostly image. For instance, the shower curtain in the bathroom is covered in crime tape, with a metal plaque near the front door which reads; 'Trespassers will be drugged and buried in the yard.'

A mannequin in the backyard holds a spade, has a silver-grey wig, glasses and wears a coat similar to the one Puente was wearing when she was arrested. It is a rather strange and ghostly tourist attraction along similar lines to the one at Monte Christo in Junee, New South Wales.

Downstairs, in the apartment where the furnace used to be, the couple have renovated the area for Barbara Holmes's mother.

Tom Williams has said that the house is quiet and free of ghosts commenting, 'If they're here, they like us. They don't say anything.'

But I note there was no word from the Chief, one of the many missing victims of: the Sacramento house of horror.

15.

THE SEX TOY STRANGLER: JAMIE LEE DOLHEGUY

'Murder is an inherently evil act,
No matter what the circumstances,
No matter how convincing the rationalisations.'
— Bentley Little

Jamie Lee Dolheguy.
PHOTOGRAPH COURTESY OF NEWS CORP

This story begins in the delightful, bushy suburb of Sunbury, which is situated some 39 kilometres (23 miles) north-west of Melbourne's central business district, in the state of Victoria. The suburb is said to be great for families, retirees and generally people who want to escape the other congested suburbs in the north and west.

Yet, it was here that the little girl, Jamie Lee Dolheguy, endured a childhood of appalling neglect and abuse, witnessing her father assaulting her mother, in front of her and her siblings. When her father was subsequently jailed, things didn't improve for young Jamie. She was sexually and physically abused time and time again. Eventually, the state stepped in and at the age of just 10, she was made a ward of the state. From the age of 14 years the traumatised teen had two carers, 24/7. Then when she turned 18, the disturbed young woman was left to live alone when the round-the-clock care was withdrawn.

It was a recipe for disaster.

■

Jamie Lee Dolheguy suffered an abusive early childhood which proved to have lasting effects on her, resulting in a troubled young woman with profound mental problems. As she had developed a personality disorder, and made a number of self-harm and suicide attempts, she began living in a Department of Health and Human Services house at 14, with two Jesuit Social Services carers who provided round-the-clock care. Amazingly, due to a supposed executive decision this care was withdrawn from February 2018, after Ms Dolheguy turned 18, leaving her living alone in the house. No doubt, feeling lonely with no functioning family as support, and needing fellow human companionship, she joined an online dating site, Plenty of Fish. Plenty of Fish is a free Canadian online dating service, primarily in Canada, but also in other countries including the United Kingdom, Ireland, Australia and New Zealand.

She was quite up-front about her situation and wrote that she was dating for the first time and had a personality disorder, had 'suicidal ideations', had self-harmed and had an interest in extreme fetishes including bondage. But she was 'happy to answer any questions'.

I guess her openness about her situation appealed to the young Indian international student, Maulin Rathod. He exchanged a series of emails, before agreeing to meet up with her saying, 'We'll do whatever you want.'

Maulin Rathod had moved to Melbourne four years earlier from India and was in the final stages of completing his Masters of Accounting degree.

Prior to her date with Maulin Rathod on 23 July 2018, Jamie Dolheguy was having a very difficult day with little or no support from her carers. Realising the situation was becoming serious, that she needed her medication saying 'there was a warzone in my head', she sent text messages to support workers saying she didn't have her medication with her saying, 'OMFG [Oh my f★★★ing God] I need it now.'

Unfortunately, the carer upset Ms Dolheguy by suggesting she go to her local pharmacy and 'enact her emergency plan' if the 'bad temptations' proved too much. Instead, while waiting for him to turn up at her home at Ross Court, Sunbury, Jamie Dolheguy went on the internet at about 7 pm and did a number of Google searches, keying in, 'I'm going to kill someone tonight help.' Following up visiting a website titled, 'Ten steps to commit murder and get away with it.'

The stage was now set for a tragedy.

■

Ms Dolheguy and Mr Rathod had never met face-to-face after connecting on Plenty of Fish. She had also sent him a number of enticing images of herself, which no doubt further interested the young man.

At 8.07 pm Maulin Rathod arrived at Ross Court, Sunbury expecting a fun evening with his new date. He was greeted at the front door by Ms Dolheguy dressed as the character Asia Lolita and escorted into the lounge room where they chatted and then 'got down to business of sexual activity'. Well, things were progressing well, as the young man expected, until Jamie Dolheguy decided on a change of play, and raised the topic of 'choke play' to supposedly heighten the sexual experience. Prior to engaging in the play, they devised a signal of tapping her on the arm when he wanted her to stop.

They climbed onto Ms Dolheguy's bed and she sat behind Mr Rathod and put him in a choke hold. Applying increasing pressure, she ignored her victim's now desperate tapping signals, along with his waving arms, reassuring him by whispering in his ear, 'It will be okay. It will be over.' Nevertheless, the strangling continued until he became a 'dead weight'. To complete the now gruesome task, she then choked him with a sex toy cord until he went limp, apparently concerned that he would regain consciousness.

Then at about 9 pm, she calmly telephoned the police and told them that she had killed a man. She told the operator, 'I strangled him. It feels so good.' But, strangely, added, 'I don't want to be a killer.'

Police arrived a short time later at Ross Court and found Mr Rathod's comatose body in Ms Dolheguy's bedroom. Paramedics arrived soon after and CPR was performed, before he was rushed to hospital. Sadly, the 24-year-old man died the next day. Jamie Dolheguy was arrested and charged with murder. In an ERISP record of interview, Ms Dolheguy told detectives she thought strangulation would be 'quick and easy' when she saw the thin build of Mr Rathod. When asked what would she have done if he had been a bigger man, she said she would have 'latched' onto his neck because she 'also had vampire fantasies'. A potentially, far more violent and blood-thirsty end for her victim.

The matter went to the Supreme Court of Victoria in Melbourne on 19 December 2019 before Justice Peter Almond. Ms Dolheguy pleaded not guilty to murder. The lawyers for Ms Dolheguy didn't dispute the fact that she killed the Indian student, but a jury of eight women and four men had to determine whether she had murderous intentions. As the lawyers made their opening addresses to the court, she sat in the dock quietly drawing on paper and colouring in with pencils.

Prosecutor Mr Patrick Bourke told the jury, Ms Dolheguy, now 20, had intended to kill Mr Rathod and used the promise of sexual activity as a trick to fulfil her deadly plan. Mr Bourke continued, 'What she did to him, what she did on the computer, what she says about it to him and to the police, she intended to kill Mr Rathod.' He further added, 'She undertook a series of steps, some preparation and plans and decisions along the way that would enable her to overpower him physically ... she needed that advantage to kill him and that's what she did.'

Defence counsel Sharon Lacy told the jury that her client was 'a much damaged young woman' who had no functioning family as support and her mental state at the time of the offence was in 'utter chaos' and she couldn't be found guilty of murder. Ms Dolheguy didn't intend for Mr Rathod to die, Ms Lacy said, and her words to the operator on the phone, that it felt 'so good', indicated her troubled mind, but she didn't intend to be a killer. Ms Lacy said to the jurors that they could find the accused guilty of manslaughter as an alternative offence to murder.

Mr Bourke gave a description of the scenario which developed saying that soon after Mr Rathod arrived at Ms Dolheguy's home they agreed for her to choke him under the guise of sexual activity, and they devised a signal if he wanted her to stop. Ms Dolheguy took Mr Rathod into her bedroom and while sitting on the bed, she got behind Mr Rathod and put him in a choke hold with her arm. But, Mr Bourke said, she ignored his tapping signal and him waving his arms and strangled him until his body became a dead weight.

Mr Bourke said prosecutors didn't have to prove a motive but that Ms Dolheguy formed an intent to kill Mr Rathod before he arrived, commenting, 'He was in the wrong place with the wrong person at the wrong time.' Concluding, 'That's it. And for her own reasons the accused killed him. The prosecution case is she intended to kill him and therefore she murdered him.'

On the following Thursday, at the Supreme Court, a jury of seven women (one female juror was discharged due to family obligations) and four men found her not guilty of murder but guilty of the alternative charge of manslaughter, after deliberating for seven days. Justice Peter Almond remanded Ms Dolheguy in custody for a pre-sentence hearing the following year.

On 22 October 2020 Jamie Lee Dolheguy, now 21, had been held in a maximum-security wing because she had a history of violence. Even there, she threatened to kill another inmate, threatened to hurt a child in front of its mother and attempted to take her own life some 25 times. Clearly a troubled young woman.

Again, she faced Supreme Court Justice Peter Almond, where the matter was reassessed for sentencing.

Justice Almond recalled that after killing Mr Rathod, Dolheguy immediately phoned police and confessed, telling them he didn't seem scared. However, the Supreme Court judge disagreed saying, 'One can only imagine the terror he felt when he realised that despite his urgent tapping, you were not going to let go.' Further adding, 'You took the life of a young person who had done nothing to harm or provoke you. He was totally trusting and unsuspecting.'

It was never in question that Ms Dolheguy had killed Mr Rathod, but her lawyers had argued she didn't intend to murder him, despite prosecutors arguing it was plain even before he arrived what she had planned.

Her barrister Sharon Lacy had said previously that Ms Dolheguy was so damaged, her mind in such chaos, that no jury could be satisfied of her murderous intent.

The jury had agreed and convicted her of manslaughter in December 2019. Back then Justice Almond was unable to take into account her severe personality disorder as a mental impairment. A forensic psychiatrist Andrew Carroll said of her, 'Because of her dreadful upbringing, she never developed a sense of basic trust in the world around her.'

Victoria's Court of Appeal only overturned its position on the disabling effects of a personality disorder in August, opening up new sentencing options in her case. Justice Almond subsequently ordered Jamie Lee Dolheguy serve a minimum of five years and six months, as she had already served two years and three months.

Aftermath: Maulin Rathod's heartbroken cousin had the miserable task of identifying his body and then to tell his parents in India what had happened to him. His parents, Hiren and Jagruti Rathod said, 'He is a victim of that girl trapping him. I [we] just hope that justice is served so this does not happen to anyone else.'

A sad end for a promising graduate student.

16.

THE WARD FOUR KILLER:
BEVERLEY GAIL ALLITT

'I deplore the horrible crime of child-murder.
We want prevention, not merely punishment.
We must reach the root of the evil, and destroy it.'
– Susan B. Anthony

Beverley Gail Allitt.

Beverley Gail Allitt was born in Grantham, United Kingdom, on 4 October 1968. She grew up in the small village of Corby Glen, which is in the South Kesteven district of Lincolnshire. It is approximately 14 kilometres (9 miles) south-east of Grantham. To all intents and purposes, Beverley had a normal upbringing along with her two sisters and a brother. Her mother worked as a school cleaner and her father worked in an off-licence (bottle shop). She left school and undertook a nursing course at Grantham College. However, early on, she began to display some disturbing tendencies, which included wearing bandages and casts over fictitious wounds that she would use to draw attention to herself.

It appeared to be the beginning of a form of Munchausen syndrome.

■

Corby Glen, is a small rural community of just over a thousand inhabitants. The delightful village is set in wooded countryside just east of the West Glen River, which flows through a valley with a distinct escarpment of Jurassic limestone surrounded by rich, gently undulating agricultural land. The area is still known as Corby to many of its residents, although the village was renamed Corby Glen in the 1950s to avoid confusion with the nearby Corby in Northamptonshire. It appears the settlement was known in Roman times with King Street and Ermine Way being the main thoroughfares through the village. In 1238 King Henry III chartered a weekly market in the village and announced an annual sheep fair. It is still held and is said to be the longest established event in the United Kingdom. A gentle, peaceful rural village.

It was in this unlikely setting that a serial murderer in the guise of a nurse who 'took care' of babies and children, was to emerge. Beverley Gail Allitt and her two sisters and a brother were raised in a normal family environment. Even so, Beverley's 1985 medical records showed a psychologically disturbed teenage woman who was prone to self-harm and had resorted to 'doctor shopping', as medical practitioners grew wise to her attention-seeking behaviours. She was admitted to hospital on a number of occasions seeking medical attention for a variety of physical ailments.

In one instance, resulting in the removal of her perfectly healthy appendix.

Beverley Allitt left school in 1987 with minimal qualifications, before commencing nurse training at Grantham College. It is said that her bizarre behaviour continued throughout her training and she had an exceptionally high level of absenteeism due to a variety of alleged 'illnesses'. However, despite her appalling record of poor class attendance and failures in her nursing examinations, she was appointed on a temporary six-month contract at the 'chronically understaffed' Grantham and Kesteven Hospital in Lincolnshire in December 1990. Here she began employment in ward four, where sick children were cared for.

For several months, Ms Allitt appeared a keen 'rookie' eager to learn the new skills. But the ward had only two trained nurses on the day shift and only one for night shift when she started her shift work.

It was a particularly cold winter evening after a significantly heavy fall of snow, on 21 February 1991, when seven-month-old Liam Taylor was admitted to the children's ward at the hospital with a chest infection.

Liam's parents were frantic, and the freezing conditions didn't help, but nurse Allitt assured them that the child was in capable hands, and persuaded them to go home and get some rest. But 'rest' was least on their minds as they were concerned for young Liam, and later returned to the hospital to check on his welfare. They were told that the child had suffered a respiratory emergency, but fortunately recovered. Nurse Allitt generously volunteered for extra night shift so she could look over the boy, and his parents chose to stay overnight at the hospital as well. It was to be a tough wintery night.

Just before midnight, Liam had another respiratory crisis, and he was alone with nurse Allitt. Initially, it appeared the boy was recovering with antibiotic treatment, only to worsen quite rapidly, suddenly suffering a cardiac arrest. Nurse Allitt alerted an emergency resuscitation team, but despite their efforts, Liam suffered brain damage and was placed on a life-support machine. Eventually, after receiving medical advice on their son's condition, his parents made the heartbreaking decision to remove him from life support. Liam Taylor's death was recorded as heart failure.

Questions were raised at the time as to why the alarms used to monitor the young patient's oxygen and breathing failed to sound when he stopped breathing. Doctors were only alerted by nurse Allitt, but by then it was too late. Nobody considered it was the rookie nurse's fault, so she continued her work unsupervised.

A fortnight later, Timothy Hardwick, an 11-year-old with cerebral palsy, was admitted to the children's ward after suffering an epileptic fit on 5 March 1991. Once again, nurse Allitt took over his care and, sadly, once again her patient relapsed, resulting in her alerting the emergency resuscitation team, who found the child turning blue (cyanosed) and an undetectable pulse. Despite their efforts, along with a paediatric specialist, the medical team were unable to revive him.

Timothy Hardwick's death was officially attributed to his epilepsy, although the post-mortem was inconclusive.

A couple of days earlier, one-year-old Kayley Desmond was admitted on 3 March 1991, with a chest infection. With antibiotic treatment the child appeared to be recovering well. Then five days later, under nurse Allitt's care, Kayley went into cardiac arrest. Ironically, in the same bed where Liam Taylor had died two weeks earlier.

Fortunately, the resuscitation team was able to revive her and she was later transferred to another hospital in Nottingham, where examining physicians found a strange puncture mark under her armpit after a thorough examination, and a large air bubble near the injection site. Curiously, no further investigations were initiated.

On 20 March 1991, five-month-old Paul Crampton attended ward four, as a result of a 'non-serious bronchial infection'. As he was about to be discharged from hospital, the child appeared to be suffering from an insulin shock, going into a near coma on three separate occasions – each time in the presence of nurse Allitt. And each time she alerted the resuscitation teams and the doctors were able to revive him, but were puzzled by the insulin levels detected. As a precaution he was transferred by ambulance to another hospital in Nottingham. Nurse Allitt travelled with him and again he was found to have too much insulin in his system. Fortunately, the doctors were *again* able to revive him and he recovered. One tough little kid!

Then on 21 March 1991, just a day after the previous incident, five-year-old Bradley Gibson was admitted to the ward suffering from pneumonia. He inexplicably went into two cardiac arrests but was saved by the resuscitation team. Again, with nurse Allitt on duty on both occasions. A blood test check for insulin revealed higher than normal levels. He was transferred to another hospital, where the child recovered.

The following day, on 22 March 1991, two-year-old Yik Hung Chan was admitted to ward four with a suspected fractured skull as the result of a fall. Nurse Allitt was in attendance when the child suffered severe anoxia (lack of oxygen) and began turning blue. Once again nurse Allitt raised the alarm and he was administered oxygen. He too, was subsequently transferred to another hospital where he recovered.

Amazingly, despite these inexplicable health incidents, all with nurse Allitt on duty, no suspicions appeared to have been aroused, apart from transferring the sick child to another hospital for further treatment which, fortunately, resulted in their survival.

The next incident concerned twins, Katie and Becky Phillips, two months old, who were kept under observation due to their premature delivery. On 1 April 1991, Becky suffered a bout of gastroenteritis and was admitted to ward four, where nurse Allitt took over her care.

Just 48 hours later, the child appeared hypoglycaemic and felt cool to touch, and nurse Allitt raised the alarm. Baby Becky was subsequently sent home to her mother. However, during the night the child went into convulsions. Sadly, the child died during the night. Doctors were concerned that whatever ailment had caused Becky's death could also affect her identical twin sister, Katie, so she was admitted to Grantham as a precaution and, unfortunately for her, to ward four, where nurse Allitt was again on duty.

It wasn't long before Katie was to suffer a similar fate to her sister. She had stopped breathing and the resuscitation team were again summoned. Eventually, efforts to revive Katie were successful, but two days later she suffered a relapse, which resulted in the collapse of her lungs. The conditions produced were later found to be due to insulin and potassium chloride overdoses.

The child was transferred to Nottingham's Queen's Medical Centre, where it was discovered that five of her ribs were broken, and worse, she had suffered serious brain damage due to oxygen deprivation. She was left epileptic and paralysed due to nurse Allitt's dubious actions. But life is full of ironies, and Katie's mother, Sue Phillips, mistakenly thinking nurse Allitt had saved her child's life, gratefully asked her to be Katie's godmother – and she accepted!

By now a sinister pattern was beginning to become evident. So when 15-month-old Claire Peck was admitted on 22 April 1991, suffering from asthma with accompanying breathing difficulties, again nurse Allitt was assigned to her case. Just after Claire began to recover, her condition worsened, she stopped breathing and suffered a heart attack. The resuscitation team revived her, but again in nurse Allitt's care, the toddler suffered a second attack. This time the resuscitation team couldn't save her.

The toddler became the fourth child to die in ward four in two months. An autopsy indicated death from 'natural causes'. It wasn't so, and tests of her blood revealed a twice the normal level of potassium in baby Clare's body. To the resident doctor, this was no coincidence.

On 30 April 1991, a now alarmed Dr Nelson Porter finally notified police.

Police Superintendent Stuart Clifton was assigned to the investigation. Suspecting foul play, he and his team of detectives examined other suspicious incidents over the previous two months. What police found was extraordinary.

But the one case that stood out was that of Paul Crampton. The baby boy had been injected with a huge dose of insulin on several occasions. The police believed nurse Allitt had injected a whole adult syringe of insulin into his tiny body. Further suspicions were raised when pages from the ward allocation log at the time of the baby boy's admission were missing and appeared ripped out. (The missing pages from the ward allocation book were later found in a drawer during a search of Beverley Allitt's house.)

During the investigation it became apparent that nurse Allitt's favoured murder weapons were syringes full of insulin or potassium chloride – drugs capable of producing lethal hypoglycaemia or cardiac arrest respectively, in her victims.

The police and prosecutors diligently built a solid case against the nurse, with experts to prove beyond doubt that the ward four deaths were not due to natural causes.

The investigation was wound up on 26 July 1991. However, it wasn't until November 1991 that Beverley Allitt was formally charged with four counts of murder, 11 cases of attempted murder and 11 cases of grievous bodily harm. It was a shocking indictment.

Further background checks revealed that her behaviour pointed to a serious personality disorder consistent with both Munchausen syndrome by proxy and Munchausen syndrome, which would give some explanation as to why she began to kill in order to satisfy her warped need to gain attention. It has been said that it is unusual for both conditions to be present in an individual.

The case aroused much media interest and so in true journalistic style, Beverley Allitt was dubbed the 'Angel of Death'.

On 15 February 1993 the matter went on trial at Nottingham Crown Court before Justice Latham, where she pleaded not guilty to the charges. During the trial the jury heard how nurse Allitt carried out injections of drugs (insulin, potassium chloride) or air, into her young victims when staff thought she was carrying out routine checks and treatments.

Prosecutors revealed to the jury how nurse Allitt had been present at each suspicious incident, and the lack of medical incidents when she was absent. Further evidence was presented relating to high readings of insulin and potassium in each of her young patient victims, along with asphyxiation of some victims, by tampering with the machines that delivered oxygen.

Professor Roy Meadow, a paediatrics expert, provided testimony relating to Ms Allitt's odd behaviour and explained to the jury about Munchausen syndrome and Munchausen syndrome by proxy, and explained how the defendant displayed symptoms of both, by providing examples of her post-arrest behaviour and the high incidence of 'illnesses', that had delayed the start of her trial.

The trial lasted almost two months, during which Beverley Allitt's numerous offences were revealed. However, she only attended 16 days due to her numerous 'illnesses'.

Beverley Allitt was convicted on Friday 28 May 1993 and given 13 life sentences for the murders and attempted murders.

After only a week in prison, where she refused to eat or drink, Beverley Allitt, was sent to Rampton Secure Hospital in Nottinghamshire, a high-security facility for high-risk individuals detained under the Mental Health Act. There she admitted in writing, to all of the 13 crimes she had been convicted of.

However, the decision to detain Beverley Allitt in Rampton is controversial. Many of the victims' families, and two notable experts, have concluded she should be in prison, not hospital. On 6 December 2007, Justice Stanely Burnton, of the High Court in London, ruled that Beverley Allitt must serve a minimum sentence of 30 years. To date she remains in Rampton.

Postscript:

Due to the damaging media coverage of the Allitt case and the shame brought upon Grantham & Kesteven Hospital the maternity unit, ward four, was closed.

In July 2018, it was reported that Beverley Allitt had contracted sepsis and was being closely monitored as she appeared close to death, but she survived this episode. In 2021 there was outrage when, during the COVID-19 crisis she was given the vaccination before her now 30-year-old victim, Katie Phillips, whom she left severely disabled and needing 24/7 care.

17.

MURDER IN A HEARTBEAT: KRISTEN HEATHER GILBERT

'The soul that has conceived one wickedness can nurse no good thereafter.'
– Sophocles

Kristen Heather Gilbert.
PHOTOGRAPH COURTESY OF YOUTUBE

Kristen Heather Strickland was born in Fall River city, Massachusetts, USA, on 13 November 1967. She was the eldest daughter of Richard and Claudia Strickland's two daughters in what appeared to be a well-adjusted home life. The family moved from Fall River to Groton, Massachusetts, about 145 kilometres (87 miles) away where her father, Richard was employed as an electronics executive and her mother, Claudia, a part-time teacher/homemaker. There Kristen lived her pre-teen years without incident.

However, when she reached her teenage years, people began to realise that something wasn't quite right with her. She became a habitual liar and had the strange habit of faking suicide attempts to manipulate people. This weird strategy continued into her college years, where she attended Bridgewater State College. The college, recognising the problem, thought she should seek psychiatric treatment. Instead, Kristen transferred to Mount Wachusett Community College followed by Greenfield Community College, where she completed her nursing degree.

A wolf was about to be released amongst the unsuspecting sheep.

■

There are some professions I believe that applicants should be psychologically screened for, despite their possibly impressive qualifications. These include police, fire brigade frontliners, teachers of children, and members of the medical profession. These professions truly impact upon the innocent and vulnerable people in our society they are supposed to assist and protect.

This case proved to be a case in point where again the checks and balances were not in place or, worse, ignored, as the previous case illustrated.

In 1988, Kristen graduated with her nursing diploma from Greenfield Community College. That same year she met Glenn Gilbert at the popular tourist destination of Hampton Beach in New Hampshire, USA. The couple hit it off and were subsequently married.

In March 1989, Kristen was offered a position at the Veterans Administration Medical Center (VAMC) in Northampton, Massachusetts, which she accepted. The young couple then bought a home and settled into their new picture-perfect life. Happy days.

Then in late 1990, after the Gilberts had their first child, a baby boy, things began to change after Kristen returned to work from maternity leave. She started working the evening shift at the hospital form 4 pm to midnight. No doubt this was a more stressful choice.

But patients started dying during this shift. Admittedly, they were elderly veterans. But there was a tripling in the medical centre's rate over the previous three years. Clearly, something was amiss. However, Nurse Kristen Gilbert was there to save the day with her calm, competent nursing skills, winning admiration and respect from her fellow workers.

After the birth of the Gilberts' second child in 1993, Kristen began a flirtatious relationship with an army veteran and night security officer at the hospital, James Perrault. By 1994, the relationship had developed into a full-blown affair with Perrault, and in the meantime she had decided to leave her husband and their young children.

But that wasn't the only drama unfolding in the V. A. Medical Centre.

A worrying increase in deaths was occurring at the VAMC and Kristen Gilbert's co-workers were beginning to get suspicious, as they always seemed to occur on her shift. Given many of the patients were old or in poor health, this was to be expected. Still, due to Kristen Gilbert being on shift for many of the serious medical episodes she was somewhat prophetically dubbed, 'The Angel of Death' by her colleagues.

There were many patients who had no medical history of heart problems, yet were dying from cardiac arrest (heart attacks). Also, a check of the medical supplies register showed a marked increase in the usage of epinephrine (adrenaline), a drug used to stimulate the heart. It is also used to treat severe allergic reactions (anaphylaxis) to insect stings (e.g. bees, wasps), foods (e.g. peanuts), drugs and other allergens.

Between late 1995 and February 1996, four patients under Nurse Gilbert's care died from heart attacks. In each case, epinephrine (adrenaline) was the suspected drug used.

In one particular incident, a Mr Stanley Jagodowski, 66 years old, was admitted for a postoperative bowel obstruction, which only needed oral medication. But an on-duty nurse saw Nurse Gilbert go into his ward room 'with a syringe in her hand'.

Mr Jagodowski died later that night.

Realising the jig was up Gilbert quit her job citing injuries she received at work. She was subsequently hospitalised after a suicide attempt where she apparently confessed to Perrault saying, 'I did it! I did it! You wanted to know? I killed all those guys by injection.'

In early September 1996, federal authorities began investigating the VAMC deaths after interviewing Perrault. Then the bomb threats began.

On 26 September, Perrault took a phone call from an anonymous person claiming to have placed three bombs at the VAMC. Evacuation of staff and patients was instigated and police notified. An extensive search was carried out but no explosives were found. Subsequent threats were during the remainder of the month with the same outcome.

All during Perrault's shifts.

Eventually, the threatening calls were traced to Kristen Gilbert. In January, 1998 she was subsequently arrested, tried and convicted of making bomb threats and sentenced to 15 months in prison. Apparently, the bomb threats were Gilbert's futile attempts to thwart the investigation into the more serious offences associated with the suspicious hospital deaths.

Meanwhile, federal investigators were sifting through medical registers and records of patients associated with Nurse Gilbert at VAMC. The evidence that was emerging proved to be quite damaging.

In November 1998, Kristen Gilbert was initially charged with three murders namely, Henry Hudon (35), Kenneth Cutting (41) and Edward Skwira (69), along with two attempted murders of Angelo Vella and Thomas Callahan. It wasn't until the following May that she was also charged with the murder of a fourth patient, Stanley Jagodowski (66) to add to her indictment.

All four of the veterans appeared to have died from cardiac arrest. But more damaging evidence came from the post-mortem examinations, three of which revealed elevated levels of epinephrine (adrenaline) in their tissues.

There was no doubt a good deal more evidence to uncover from another 37 deaths out of 63 patients that had occurred in Ward C when Nurse Gilbert was on duty. The matter still went to Northampton Court in November 2000 with Kristen Gilbert being only indicted with four murders and two attempted murders of patients admitted to the Veterans Affairs Medical Center, Northampton, Massachusetts.

The court prosecutors, William Welch, and Ariane Vuono, in their opening addresses said that Kristen Gilbert committed the murders to get the attention from her peers associated with medical emergencies and most likely also to impress her boyfriend, James Perrault. It was estimated that over a seven-year span, she was on duty for half of 350 deaths that occurred in Ward C.

The moniker 'Angel of Death' now appeared to be justified.

In closing arguments, prosecutors said that Kristen Gilbert used the 'perfect poison' (epinephrine) to murder her victims: 'They were vulnerable. They were perfect victims. When Kristen Gilbert killed them, she used the perfect poison.'

In some ways, it was the perfect poison – and one that occurs naturally. The human body reacts to excitement in much the same way it reacts to feelings of stress or fear (fight or flight syndrome): by releasing the hormone epinephrine (adrenaline). This in turn, can trigger cardiac arrest and strokes, along with other potentially fatal medical emergencies through overstimulation of the heart. No doubt, nurse Kristen Gilbert would have been aware of this.

Defence lawyers for Gilbert argued that she was innocent and that her patients had died from natural causes.

Well, the poison was *natural!*

Defence lawyer David Hoose then introduced the possible repercussions of an extramarital affair by saying to the jury, 'She was scorned by her peers and her co-workers. You must understand how rumours about what was going on in Kristen Gilbert's life affected, colored and tainted everyone's opinions of what was going on in Ward C.'

This defence and other factors presented were found unacceptable by the federal jury and on 14 March 2001, Kristen Gilbert was found guilty of three counts of first degree murder, one count of second degree murder and two counts of attempted murder.

Then on 26 March 2001 the jury recommended life imprisonment without parole, as Massachusetts does not have the death penalty. The following day, the judge formally sentenced Kristen Gilbert to four consecutive life terms without the possibility of parole, plus 20 years. (As Gilbert's crimes were carried out on federal property, she qualified for the death penalty by lethal injection. It would have been an ironic end to her life given the nature of her crimes.)

Kristen Gilbert was subsequently incarcerated at the Federal Medical Centre (FMC Carswell) in Fort Worth, Texas, where she is currently serving her sentence.

In July 2003 Kristen Gilbert appealed for a new trial, which was promptly dropped when the US Supreme Court ruled that would have permitted prosecutors to pursue the death penalty upon retrial. Not surprisingly, things have gone very quiet.

18.

MURDER BY INSULIN:
THE MEGAN HAINES CASE

'Be careful who you trust, the devil was once an angel.'
– Anon

Megan Haines.
PHOTOGRAPH COURTESY OF *THE NORTHERN STAR*

Ballina is a delightful seaside village on the far north coast of New South Wales. Located 737 kilometres (442 miles) north of Sydney via the Pacific Highway, it's only 90 kilometres (54 miles) from the Queensland border. With eight superb beaches, it's a haven for surfers and tourists alike.

But Ballina isn't all about beaches because this scenic seaside town also plays host to a number of quality aged nursing homes, including the St Andrew's Village aged-care facility, in which this story unfolds. St Andrew's is a privately operated nursing home with some 117 residents (at the time of writing), and it offers care levels ranging from low-care hostel-type accommodation to high-care nursing home facilities. Residents occupy their own rooms and are cared for by nursing and care staff. The facility operates round-the-clock, seven days a week, and has staff to cover each of the three daily shifts – morning, afternoon and night.

But quality care, depends upon quality staff.

■

Marie Darragh, 82, Isabella Spencer, 77 and 88-year-old Marjorie 'Madhi' Patterson were residents of the St Andrew's Village high-care nursing facilities known as the Dianella 1 and Dianella 2 wings. Marie Darragh and Isabella Spencer were in Dianella 1 wing, while Marjorie Patterson was in the adjoining Dianella 2 wing. Apart from Isabella, who had type 2 diabetes, all three residents just had the usual medical ailments associated with old age, such as cardiac conditions, arthritis and other associated problems.

On the evening of Friday 9 May 2014, Megan Haines (previously known as Megan Dickson), a registered nurse (RN) and divorced single mother of two dependent children, Ashely, aged 12, and Zack, aged 4, began her night shift at St Andrew's Village at about 10 pm. On duty with her was a care service employee (CSE), Marlene Ridgeway, who had been at the facility for a number of years and had been working the night shift in the Dianella wing for about 12 months. Three other CSE staff were also in the facility in various other areas, although being the RN, Megan Haines was the one in charge and therefore the one who was responsible for the administration of medication to patients on that shift.

At about 11 pm that evening, the Director of Care, Wendy Turner, visited St Andrew's Village and met with Megan Haines, handing her written notification that complaints had been made against her. Furthermore, she was informed that the complaints had been lodged by Marie Darragh and Marjorie Patterson. Arrangements were made for a further meeting to be held the following Tuesday. It looked like Megan Haines's job could be on the line.

Wendy Turner left the facility around 11.40 pm and Megan Haines returned to her RN duties in the Dianella Wing, no doubt seething from the news. But duty called. Just after midnight, Marlene Ridgeway left Megan Haines alone in the Dianella Wing, as she was required in another part of the nursing home to assist other staff, returning after about an hour so they could begin their joint round. Before they started, they visited Marie Darragh's room, where they heard groaning noises. They listened for a while with Megan Haines commenting, 'Oh, she's just having a dream.'

The two of them then went on to minister to the various residents, with Megan Haines seeing to Isabella Spencer and Marlene Ridgeway seeing to a neighbouring resident.

After completing the round at about 2.20 am, Megan Haines told Marlene Ridgeway about the two complaints against her and talked about how it may affect her nursing registration. They then went to the nurse's station, where they attended to general administration duties and answered resident call-button requests as needed.

Before beginning the second round of the night, they signed out Schedule 8 medication for a resident. During the round, Megan Haines indicated that Isabella Spencer was fine. However, no checks were made on Marie Darragh or Marjorie Patterson. The round was completed at about 6 am when their shift concluded, and they handed over to the day staff, which comprised an RN and her CSEs, who later found both Marie Darragh and Isabella Spencer sweating heavily in an unconscious state.

The RN promptly contacted Dr Jerome Mellor, the on-call doctor, for advice. He prescribed pain care and advised that both patients be transferred to Ballina Hospital, saying that he'd come to oversee the transfer and make examinations of the two women. However, before the transfer could be made, both Marie Darragh and Isabella Spencer passed away in the presence of their families and friends.

Meanwhile, Marjorie Patterson complained to Dr Mellor and the St Andrew's Village staff that she'd been awoken during the night by Megan Haines and given unscheduled pain medications, so she was transferred to Ballina Hospital for further observation and blood tests.

Due to the circumstances and the unexpected deaths of Marie Darragh and Isabella Spencer, death certificates were not issued and the matter was referred to the police for further investigation.

Later the same day, it was determined that an open ampoule of Mixtard 30/70 insulin, prescribed for resident Edward Capewell (a diabetes sufferer), was missing from the medication room in the Dianella wing. Subsequently, police set up and secured crime scene areas in the rooms where Marie Darragh and Isabella Spencer had been residents and in the Dianella wing medication rooms. Crime scene examinations were carried out after a warrant had been granted by Parramatta Local Court. On completion of those examinations, the bodies of both Marie Darragh and Isabella Spencer were transferred to Lismore Base Hospital morgue.

On 11 May, prior to their transfer to the Department of Forensic Medicine in Newcastle for post-mortems, several sets of blood samples were taken from the two deceased women to be analysed for insulin and C-peptide concentrations. The post-mortems were completed by Dr Vuletic on 13 May, but he was unable to establish a cause of death for either of the women. Additionally, no natural causes of death could be established. Further blood samples were taken.

A blood sample taken from Marie Darragh's post-mortem in Lismore was found to have present frusemide less than 1 milligram per litre, morphine (free) 0.03 milligrams per litre, morphine-3-glucuronide 0.05 milligrams per litre, paracetamol less than 5 milligrams per litre and temazepam 0.02 milligrams per litre. Likewise, a blood sample in Newcastle, taken from the same woman at post-mortem, was found to have present morphine (free) 0.02 milligrams per litre, morphine-3-glucuronide 0.06 milligrams per litre, paracetamol less than 5 milligrams per litre and temazepam 0.02 milligrams per litre.

Frusemide (also known as furosemide) is a sulphonamide-type drug which is used as a diuretic and antihypertensive. It's available under the trade name Lasix and is used in the treatment of oedema and fluid retention.

Morphine is an opiate analgesic for the treatment of moderate to severe pain. The usual dosage of morphine to treat pain in adults is between 5 and 20 milligrams, given by injection every four hours if needed. However, an individual with heightened reflex excitability of their nervous system may take two to three times the ordinary dose and suffer few, if any, side effects. For example, a patient with severe pain from renal colic or coronary disease may be given 45–60 milligrams of morphine before pain relief is obtained and their respiration won't be seriously affected.

Generally, the toxic dose of morphine for a non-addicted person is somewhere in the region of 60 milligrams, and serious symptoms are usually experienced after doses of 100 milligrams. A therapeutic dose of morphine ranging from 5 to 20 milligrams (average 10 milligrams) in a 70-kilogram adult produces a blood morphine concentration of 0.04 to 0.10 milligrams per litre, whereas, 55–65 milligrams of morphine taken intravenously can result in a blood morphine concentration ranging between 0.8 and 2.6 milligrams per litre, leading to profound respiratory depression. The therapeutic range for morphine is given as 0.05–0.12 mg/L. Marie Darragh's blood morphine (free) level was 0.03 mg/L and morphine-3-glucuronide 0.05 milligrams per litre, which indicated she'd received a therapeutic dosage for pain relief.

Paracetamol (acetaminophen) is an analgesic (pain relief) and antipyretic (fever lowering) drug used in the symptomatic management of moderate to mild pain and fever associated with illnesses such as colds and influenza. It's often combined with other drugs, especially codeine, to provide stronger pain relief. The usual adult dose, administered orally, is between 500 and 1000 milligrams every four to six hours, up to a maximum of 4 grams (4000 milligrams) daily. The blood concentration of paracetamol was less than the therapeutic range (10–20 mg/L) and indicated that the drug had been ingested sometime earlier.

Temazepam is a benzodiazepine-type sedative which is available under several trade names, including Normison, and is used for short-term management of insomnia in adults. The blood concentration of temazepam was less than the therapeutic range (0.3–0.9 mg/L) and, once again, indicated that the drug had been taken sometime earlier.

The blood sample taken from Isabella Spencer at ante-mortem was found to have present gliclazide less than 1 milligram per litre, temazepam 0.05 milligrams per litre, oxazepam 0.005 milligrams per litre, sertraline 0.14 milligrams per litre and paracetamol less than 5 milligrams per litre.

A further sample taken at post-mortem was found to have present gliclazide less than 1 milligram per litre, temazepam 0.06 milligrams per litre, oxazepam less than 0.005 milligrams per litre, sertraline 0.08 milligrams per litre and paracetamol less than 5 milligrams per litre.

Gliclazide is a sulfonylurea derivative, which in turn is an oral hypoglycaemic drug. It's available under various trade names such as Glygard, Glyzide, Glucomed, Nordialex and Diamicron, and is used for the treatment of non-insulin dependent diabetes mellitus where the blood sugar (glucose) is higher than normal. The therapeutic blood concentration of gliclazide was 0.7–4.9 mg/L, which indicated the drug had been ingested sometime earlier.

Oxazepam is a pharmacologically active metabolite of temazepam as well as a drug in its own right. The blood concentration of temazepam was less than the therapeutic range (0.3–0.9 mg/L) and indicated that the drug had also been taken sometime earlier.

Sertraline is a selective serotonin re-uptake inhibitor (SSRI) anti-depressant which can result in dizziness and drowsiness, and so care should be taken with any activity that requires alertness and judgement, particularly early in treatment. It's available under the trade name Zoloft and is used to treat anxiety and depression. The blood concentration of sertraline was within the therapeutic range (0.05–0.25mg/L) and again indicated the drug had been ingested sometime earlier.

The blood concentration of paracetamol was also less than the therapeutic range (10–20 mg/L), once more an indication that the drug had been taken sometime earlier.

The upshot of all of the above is that the medications administered to Marie Darragh and Isabella Spencer appeared to be consistent with the hospital records and the needs of the respective patients.

However, the endocrinology and glucose results for the two deceased women were inconsistent and provided a different story.

A blood sample taken from Marie Darragh on 11 May was found to have present insulin 134 H mIU/L (milli–international units per litre)[<=9] and C-peptide 0.08 L nmol/L (nanomoles per litre)[0.26–1.73].

A vitreous humour sample taken from her and tested on 12 May was found to have present glucose less than 0.3 mmol/L, while a blood sample taken from her and tested on 16 May was found to have present insulin 2 H mIU/L [<=9] and C-peptide <0.05 L nmol/L [0.26–1.73]. A urine sample tested on 20 June was found to have present glucose less than 0.11 mmol/L. Essentially, Marie Darragh's blood glucose level was *too* low.

A blood sample taken from Isabella Spencer on 11 May was found to have present insulin 53 H mIU/L [<=9] and C-peptide 0.05 L nmol/L [0.26–1.73], while a further blood sample taken from her and tested on 20 June was found to have present insulin 1 H mIU/L [<=9] and C-peptide <0.05 L nmol/L [0.26–1.73]. A urine sample tested on the same date was found to have present glucose 0.4 mmol/L.

Insulin is a peptide protein hormone which is produced naturally by the pancreas and regulates the metabolism of carbohydrates and fats in the body by promoting the absorption of glucose from the blood to skeletal muscles. Excess carbohydrates are stored as glycogen, mainly in the liver and muscles, and any carbohydrates that cannot be stored as glycogen are converted by insulin into fats and stored in the adipose (fatty) tissues. Insulin also promotes the uptake of amino acids and their subsequent conversion into protein. It's present in the body at a constant level in order to remove excess glucose from the blood.

When the blood glucose levels fall below a certain level, the body begins to use the stored sugar (in the form of glycogen stored in the liver and muscle) as an energy source through a process known as glycogenolysis. However, when the blood glucose falls too low (into the range of 20–

50 milligrams per decilitre (mg/100 mL), symptoms of hypoglycaemic shock develop. They include double or blurry vision, headache, hunger, shaking or trembling and progressive nervous irritability, which lead to fainting, seizures, sweating, shallow breathing, hypotension and coma. Insulin overdosage (insulin shock) causes hypoglycaemia, the treatment of which generally involves the administration of glucose or glucagon.

The initial insulin levels found in the deceased women were as follows:

Marie Darragh

134 H mIU/L (milli-International Units per litre), blood sampled on 1 May, the day after her death. A follow-up sample taken on 16 May showed an insulin level of 2 H mIU/L.

Isabella Spencer

53 H mIU/L, blood sampled on 11 May, the day after her death. A follow-up sample taken on 20 June was found to still have present insulin 1 H mIU/L.

Insulin has been used as a means of committing homicide in the past, and given the elevated insulin levels detected in both of the deceased, it was felt prudent to measure the level serum C-peptide in their blood. Serum C-peptide is an inactive remnant of exogenous proinsulin, and it can provide an indication of exogenous insulin administration.

The serum level of C-peptide is normally within the range of 0.7–3.3 ng/ml, and an elevated value for the insulin/C-peptide molar concentration in post-mortem blood does not generally exceed 1.0. It's therefore seen as a useful indicator of exogenous insulin injection. However, the time of testing should take place within 24–48 hours of the post-mortem because C-peptide degrades more rapidly than insulin.

The initial C-peptide levels detected in the deceased were:

Marie Darragh

C-peptide 0.08 L nmol/L (nanomoles per litre), blood sampled on 11 May, the day after her death.

Isabella Spencer

C-peptide 0.05 L nmol/L, blood sampled on 11 May, the day after her death.

Marie Darragh was being treated by Dr Chris Greenway for a variety of medical conditions, including cardiac problems, pruritus (itching), arthritis and back pain, but not diabetes (type 1 or 2). Isabella Spencer was being treated by Dr Colin McDonald for a variety of medical conditions, including right myocardial infarction, left hemiplegia (stroke), urinary incontinence, hypertension, renal calculi, dysphagia and diabetes mellitus type 2.

More importantly, neither patient was an insulin-dependent diabetic. However, Marie Spencer was taking the oral anti-diabetic drug gliclazide for treatment of her type 2 diabetes.

Following discussions with other experts in the area, I concluded that given the amount of insulin detected in both the deceaseds' blood, together with the presence of C-peptide/glucose levels in both incidents, it appeared to be consistent with fatal doses of insulin administration.

As events unfolded, I wasn't called to give evidence on that matter, only on whether the other medication given at the nursing home to both of the deceased had been appropriate. After closely inspecting their medical records, I soon realised that the other nursing staff of the Dianella wing had carried out their duties according to the patients' needs and hospital protocol. The fly in the ointment truly was Megan Haines RN.

In the meantime, the police had been very busy. Strike Force Odimi had been formed to investigate the suspicious deaths, with Odimi standing for versatility, enthusiasm, agility and unconventional methods.

Megan Jean Dickson Haines RN was subsequently arrested after being extradited from the southern Victorian town of Seaspray, and charged with the aged-care-home murders.

The matter then went before Justice Peter Garling in the Supreme Court in Sydney on 3 November 2016. Evidence was presented to show that on 9 May 2014, within a month of Megan Haines starting her new job at the St Andrew's Village aged care facility, three elderly residents had complained about her, and the following morning two of them had been found dead.

The jury also heard some details about Megan Haines's eventful nursing career, which included three prior professional misconduct findings in Victoria. The Crown also alleged that she realised that another complaint investigation could be potentially disastrous for her career, given her past misconduct findings.

Following a two-and-a-half-week trial, it took the jury just a few hours to find her guilty on two counts of murder. She showed no emotion as the verdict was read out.

But more was to follow.

The jury hadn't been made aware of the full details of Haines's chequered history, namely the ins and outs of the previous damning misconduct findings, with alleged drug convictions, assault of patients, theft of jewellery investigations, and previous insulin misuse allegations, which had been picked up following routine blood tests that had detected the presence of elevated insulin levels in two elderly patients at Box Hill Hospital, Melbourne, Victoria, in early 2008.

In addition, jewellery of both patients had gone missing and the only nurse on duty in the ward at that time had been Haines. Police had searched her home in the suburb of Boronia, but failed to find the pieces, so nothing had come of the investigation. No doubt, the jewellery had been pawned off. They had, however, found a small amount of cannabis, and had brought a charge for drug possession.

Sadly, suspicion had fallen on all the nursing staff, until investigations subsequently revealed Haines to be implicated.

In February 2008, Haines had been stripped of her registration by the Nursing Board of Victoria due to misconduct, and when she'd applied to have it reinstated a year later, she'd been refused because a third misconduct investigation had still been in progress.

She'd made another application for her registration in 2012 after legislation had changed the watchdog system from a state to a federal model, and on that occasion, she'd been successful. That, of course, had set in motion the chain of events that had led to the two murders.

Sentencing was set for the NSW Supreme Court on 16 December 2016. Megan Haines sat in the accused box as her sentence was handed down. She alternated between looking up at Justice Peter Garling and down at the floor, never making eye contact with the family members of the victims.

Justice Garling stated the Megan Haines's actions amounted to '... conduct almost too awful to contemplate and cannot be tolerated.' Adding, 'Her conduct was deliberate and calculating. It was a gross breach of trust and flagrant abuse of her power. She clearly abused that position of trust. I consider this to be a significant aggravating factor.'

The then 49-year-old Megan Haines was given a maximum sentence of 36 years in jail, with a minimum of 27 years. She will be eligible for parole in 2041. By then, she will be almost as old as her youngest victim, Isabella Spencer.

Rodney Spencer, Isabella's brother, was so overcome with emotion that he had to leave the court. On departing, he said, 'I knew I'd lose a sister sooner or later, but not in those circumstances, and listening to what the judge said, it started to get to me,' as tears started to well up in his eyes. But he was very pleased with the sentence Megan Haines received.

The chief executive of St Andrew's aged care facility said that the former nurse's sentence acknowledged the pain and suffering that had been endured by the family and friends of the victims.

Could these tragic events that unfolded have been prevented? Most possibly.

Ms Haines received a second chance to sort out her life before it again impacted on the elderly. She had a tarnished background before being appointed to the nursing staff at St Andrew's Village aged care facility, Ballina. A routine background check would have revealed her dubious past.

So, who was responsible for the appointment of the nurse? The medical board? The nurse's registration board? Or the Health Care Complaints Commission? In reality, probably all of them. With better communication, the true nature of the nurse's questionable background would have been known and appropriate preventative action could have been taken before even more serious offences were committed.

Were lessons learned from this case?

Hopefully, yes, for all professionals concerned and for the better treatment any future elderly patients that may come under the 'care' of less than caring medical professionals.

How Megan Haines will fare during her term in prison is anyone's guess, as prison inmates generally consider it to be 'a dog act' to kill old ladies.

I can't disagree.

19.

THE CURRY KILLING: LAKHVIR KAUR SINGH

'There is poison in the fang of a serpent;
In the mouth of the fly and in the sting of a scorpion;
But the wicked person is saturated with it.'
– Chanakya

Lakhvir Kaur Singh.

Aconitine is one of a number of highly poisonous alkaloids present in the toxic plant genus *Aconitum*. A number of *Aconitum* species contain significant amounts of aconitine and related alkaloids. The alkaloid is present in the leaves, stem and root of *Aconitum* sp. The toxic aconite plants include various species such as *Aconitum napellus,* which is more commonly known as monkshood or wolfsbane, and *Aconitum carmichaelii,* better known as Chinese aconite or Chinese wolf's bane. Toxins extracted from the plants were traditionally used to kill wolves, hence the name 'wolf's bane'. However, most of the 250 or so species are very poisonous and must be handled with care.

Chinese wolf's bane has been used in Chinese herbal medicine for treatment of a variety of ailments, including skin diseases, rheumatism, arthritis, cold hands and feet, deficiency in kidneys, body aches and all 'yang-injuries'. The usual dosage is between 3 and 8 grams. However, the fresh drug is very poisonous, although it becomes somewhat less toxic after drying. Nevertheless, it should be brewed for a long time.

The alkaloid generally held responsible for the plant's toxic properties is aconitine, although the less potent hypaconitine, jesaconitine and mesaconitine are also poisonous.

Various toxic symptoms due to aconite ingestion include nausea, vomiting, numbness and palsy of the extremities. Other symptoms include diarrhoea, difficulty in breathing and cardiac arrhythmia. Death may occur from paralysis of the heart or the respiratory centre.

Aconitine has been known as the Queen of Poisons and has featured in a number of notable deaths throughout history, including that of George Henry Lamson in 1882. He was a doctor, and he went from being a decorated war hero who served with distinction during the wars that ravaged Europe and the Balkans to being a bankrupt drug addict and murderer. During the war in Romania and Serbia, he served his time as a surgeon, returning to England, where he practised in Bournemouth. Unfortunately, he became addicted to morphine, and that addiction drained his finances so badly that he became desperate for money.

It was then that he decided to use the Queen of Poisons to murder his disabled 18-year-old brother-in-law, Percy Malcolm, for an inheritance of £3000, a princely sum in those days. He visited Percy at his boarding school and gave him a slice of Dundee cake, along with a capsule that was later tested and found to contain aconitine. He was eventually arrested and tried in March 1882 at the Old Bailey and found guilty of murder. The following month, he was hanged in Wandsworth Prison.

Another death attributable to aconitine poisoning was that of 25-year-old Canadian actor Andre Noble, who died in 2004 when he apparently mistook a monkshood for an edible flower during a hiking trip with his aunt on Fair Island, Newfoundland. He became very ill at her cabin near Centreville, Indian Bay, and later died while being conveyed to hospital.

More recently, in 2009, another notorious aconitine poisoning occurred.

Dubbed by the media as the 'Curry Killer' case, it centred on Lakhvir Kaur Singh, aged 45, her lover of 16 years, Lakhvinder Cheema, aged 39 and a beautiful young Indian woman, Ms Gurjeet Choongh, 21 years old.

It truly was a tragic case of a love triangle with fatal results.

■

This story begins in Southall, West London, a district often referred to as 'Little Punjab' or 'Little India', which has been a South Asian hub since the 1950s. Southall Market on High Street sells a huge variety of produce ranging from spices and vegetables, both exotic and local, to jewellery and antiques. While restaurants and various eateries along The Broadway offer a variety of delicious Indian cuisine. Southall also has one of the largest Sikh temples outside India, Gurdwara Sri Guru Singh Sabha.

The suburb is considered a great place to live for London's Indian population, where it is easy to get the best food, clothing and home comforts of mother India.

It was in this setting that this tragic story of betrayal and murder unfolds.

Mr Lakhvinder 'Lucky' Cheema, was employed as a cleaner and was having serious family problems. Eventually, his marriage failed and after divorce settlements, he had little option but to move into his elder brother's home in Southall. Initially, it was an amicable arrangement with Uncle Lakhvinder getting along well with his three nephews.

Unfortunately, Mrs Lakhvir Kaur Singh, who was 'trapped in a loveless marriage', arranged when she as only 20 years old, saw an opportunity to improve her love life and set out to seduce their young new tenant.

She succeeded. The affair continued for 16 years, even while her husband, Aunkar, 57, was receiving various treatments for cancer. Mr Cheema eventually moved out and bought his own home; still their clandestine lovers' meetings continued. During this time Mrs Lakhvir Singh became pregnant on two occasions, but each time her lover made her have an abortion, fearful of the shame that their affair would bring on them should it be discovered. Even so, for years Mrs Lakhvir Singh visited his house every day to cook, clean and do his laundry like a devoted wife.

Sadly, for Mrs Lakhvir Singh this blissful relationship was about to end.

It was in the form of a beautiful young Indian woman, albeit an illegal immigrant, Gurjeet Choongh. Lakhvinder 'Lucky' Cheema was besotted with her and they soon became lovers and engaged.

Lakhvir Kaur Singh, aged 45, was now filled with jealousy and rage towards her former lover of 16 years, Lakhvinder Cheema, 39. To add to her misery she found him in bed with his fiancée one morning on her 'house wifely duties'.

That clinched it, and she threatened to burn down his house.

Lakhvir then bombarded him with text messages begging him to break off the engagement, describing him as a 'bastard' and declaring her heart was broken. Nevertheless, Lakhvinder and his now fiancée Gurjeet Choongh planned to get married just weeks away, on Valentine's Day no less, and hoped to start a family.

But when Mr Cheema refused to break off the engagement, Lakhvir Kaur Singh was prepared to kill rather than share him with anyone else (despite being married with three children).

A cruel revenge was now afoot using the plant aconite, or wolf's bane, a deadly ancient toxin known. A trip to India provided her 'the ancient choice of poisoners' – a poison supposedly used by witches in the Middle Ages. On 27 January 2008, desperate to prevent their forthcoming marriage on Valentine's Day, Mrs Singh broke into the house in Feltham, Middlesex that Lakhvinder Cheema now shared with his fiancée, and spiked a prepared chicken curry in the fridge with Indian aconite (*Aconitium ferox*).

When the couple returned home, they settled down for their evening meal, unaware the food had been poisoned. Lakhvinder (also ironically known as 'Lucky') was very hungry and tucked into a second helping. Fortunately, his fiancée only had a small portion.

Within minutes, the couple experienced the toxic effects of the poison. Before Lakhvinder fell unconscious, he said he suspected Lakhvir Singh of the foul deed because an attempt on his life had been made some time earlier and after calling 999, said to the operator, 'Someone put poison in our food. She is my ex-girlfriend.'

Shortly after, he began to lose vision and control of his arms and legs crying out to his beloved fiancée, 'Please help.'

It was a desperate situation – and the paramedics still hadn't turned up.

A decision was made by family members to take the now violently ill man by car to hospital rather than waiting for an ambulance. On the way, in a gentle gesture, Miss Choongh tried to reach for her fiancés hand as they were taken to hospital, but she too was paralysed by the poison.

Mr Cheema eventually lapsed into unconsciousness in hospital and died soon after.

Ms Gurjeet Choongh was placed in a medically induced coma to stabilise her heartbeat and survived, probably because of her youth and because she had eaten less of the poisoned meal.

In the meantime police were notified and carried out their investigations into the matter. As Mrs Lakhvir Singh was considered a prime suspect, a search was made of her home in Southall, where detectives found two bags of dried herbs in her coat and handbag. When questioned about the stash, Mrs Singh claimed the herbs were used for a 'neck rash' she allegedly suffered.

The herbs were subsequently submitted to a forensic laboratory where, on testing, they were found to contained the deadly alkaloid, aconite or more accurately, aconitine, which matched the poison found in the curry.

Aconitine, like cyanide, stops the heart and other internal organs from working, resulting in death from asphyxiation. Prior to death, victims suffer from severe vomiting, clammy skin, tingling of the hands and feet and the awful sensation of ants crawling over their body and their breathing becomes shallower. Eventually, victims lose the power to control their limbs, but the mind still remains clear throughout the ordeal, making this poison a particularly cruel death.

Mrs Lakhvir Singh was charged with murder and attempted murder.

On 11 February 2010 the matter went on trial at the Old Bailey court before Justice Paul Worsley. The court was told of Mrs Lakhvir Singh's 16-year affair with Mr Lakhvinder 'Lucky' Cheema after his first marriage had failed, and the events leading up to the murder of Mr Cheema after he broke off the affair to marry a much younger woman, Ms Gurjeet Choongh, in October 2008. The spurned woman had then planned her revenge. This despite being married with three children. She was filled with jealousy and rage and planned to kill Lucky rather than share him with someone else.

After a trip to India, she set about poisoning her former lover and his new fiancée with the deadly ancient herb, Indian aconite (*Aconitium ferox*) which she sprinkled into a chicken curry stored in a refrigerator, knowing that he and his fiancée were planning to eat the meal that evening.

Even so, Lakhvir Singh tried unsuccessfully to blame her brother-in-law, Varinda for the murder. However, two lodgers saw her take the curry out of the refrigerator and 'putting something' into it. The poison in the curry matched the herbal preparation found in Mrs Singh's possession. Evidence was presented that the cause of Mr Cheema's death was due to aconite (aconitine), from the plant, *Aconitium ferox* – which means 'ferocious' aconite in Latin. An appropriate name.

Eventually, after a number of witnesses and victim impact statements, Mrs Lakhvir Kaur Singh was found guilty of murder and also found guilty of causing Ms Gurjeet Choongh grievous bodily harm with intent. However, she was cleared of attempting to murder Ms Choongh and of the prior administration of a poison to Mr Cheema in December 2008 at his residence in Princes Road, Feltham, West London.

In sentencing her at the Old Bailey, Justice Paul Worsley said to her, 'You were not just a spurned lover, you did not simply explode in anger at your rejection. You set about a cold and calculating revenge.'

The Crown had sought life imprisonment for Lakhvir Singh with a minimum term of 30 years, due to the gravity of the case and the level of premeditation involved along with the fact two victims were involved.

Mrs Lakhvir Kaur Singh was sentenced to life imprisonment with a minimum term of 23 years. This case resulted in Mrs Lakhvir Singh achieving the dubious distinction of becoming the first person to be convicted of murder using the rare poison since 1882.

20.

THE ICE CREAM KILLER: ESTIBALIZ CARRANZA

'No place indeed should murder sanctuarize;
Revenge should have no bounds.'
– William Shakespeare

Estibaliz Carranza.
PHOTOGRAPH COURTESY OF *THE DAILY MAIL*

This is another infamous murder case which involved an attractive woman by the name of Goidsargi Estibaliz Carranza Zabala or more commonly, Estibaliz Carranza, who was the owner of the Schleckeria ice-cream parlour in Vienna, Austria. Here was a highly intelligent woman driven by one goal in life – to have a child. On the surface, a very natural quest for a young woman. But unfortunately, the men in her life could not or would not deliver.

Simple solution, she murdered them, cutting up their bodies with a chainsaw and disposing of the body parts in the basement coldroom used for the ice-cream shop.

■

This story begins in Vienna the capital of Austria, which lies east of the Danube River. It is a delightful city, considered amongst the most liveable in the world, and hosts a variety of attractions including its imperial palaces such as the Schönbrunn, the Habsburgs' summer residence.

The city's musical, artistic and intellectual legacies were moulded by notable residents such as Beethoven, Mozart and Sigmund Freud. A very sophisticated, beautiful and affluent city.

Goidsargi Estibaliz Carranza Zabala or Estibaliz Carranza, a Mexican-born Spanish national, was a very bright young lady who gained top honours at university, becoming fluent in Italian, Spanish, English and German. To improve her job prospects she travelled to Germany. Given her intelligence and abilities she could have had a very successful professional career. Instead, her main goal in life was to be a mother, and to get some experience in looking after children she gained work as an au pair.

After taking on a job as an ice-cream parlour waitress, she met and married her first husband, Holger Holz, 36. She was 22 and eager to have a large family.

It wasn't to be a happy marriage.

She recalled later saying, 'As he put the ring on my finger I was crying inside. I knew I had made a mistake.' While Estibaliz had aspirations to become a mother, the potential father proved to be violent and lazy. Not good qualities for a future dad.

However, Holz promised her they would start a family if they moved to Vienna to run an ice-cream parlour, the Schleckeria in the Wien-Meidling district of Vienna. Unfortunately, things only got worse after the move. Eventually, Estibaliz filed for divorce and was successful in her application in 2008. Not willing to accept the outcome, Holger Holz refused to move out of the residence after their divorce.

The scene was now set for a series of murders.

The first was triggered, when Holger Holz was busy at the computer playing games and Estibaliz Carranza was dressed up ready to have a date with a man she had met online.

When Holz made an inappropriate – and fatal, remark, 'Esti, give up looking – you are never going to find another man.'

That was it, she was furious.

Nearby, there were four guns on a table (Holger Holz was a gun enthusiast and collector), Estibaliz took one of them, a loaded .22 Beretta pistol. She aimed the weapon at the back of her husband's head and fired off three rounds. After the body finished twitching, she went out, and spent the night with the man she had met online.

Yes, she had found another man.

On returning home the following morning she was confronted with the blood-covered body of her former husband – and now faced the daunting problem of disposal of the gruesome evidence. Dousing his dead body with a flammable liquid, Schnapps (no less!), proved to be ineffective and only raised the attention from the local fire brigade due to the amount of smoke generated. When the fire brigade turned up, Estibaliz refused to let them in saying she had burnt some food and the problem had been dealt with. Amazingly, the firies accepted her explanation and simply left without any further inquiries.

Realising she had a serious problem of body disposal, she purchased a chainsaw to cut the body into pieces. She then hacked his dead body apart with a chainsaw and stored his various parts in the basement freezer, only to find 'the smell would not go away,' she then transferred the body parts into ice-cream tubs filled with concrete mix. With the addition of air freshers, the problem was solved.

Two years were to pass, and things seemed to return to some degree of normality. Estibaliz Carranza now rekindled a previous affair she had with an ice-cream-machine salesman, Manfred Hinterberger, 48, some 20 years her senior.

But Manfred had a roving eye. He had been quite happy to be involved earlier with her in an extramarital affair, but now chose to be unfaithful to her. The discovery of pornographic pictures of other women including a number of suggestive text messages didn't improve Manfred's relationship with Estibaliz. He was doomed.

Furious, she went back to the same hardware store and purchased the same equipment she had used a couple of years earlier to dispose of Holger Holz's body. In the meantime, she recovered the Beretta pistol from the cellar where she had hidden it along with Mr Holz's remains.

Later that night, while Manfred and Estibaliz were lying in bed, unable to sleep through his snoring, she got up and went into the entrance hall where she had left the pistol and placed it under the mattress. A quick check of the cartridge chamber of the weapon showed there were sufficient bullets to carry out the foul deed. Estibaliz went back to the bedroom, where Manfred was sleeping and still snoring heavily. She aimed the weapon at the back of his head and fired off four rounds.

A familiar story – and end.

But this time she knew how to dispose of this dead body without the accompanying problems experienced with the previous murder. She bought large sheets of plastic and covered everything in the room. Then, with the chainsaw, she cut up the body into pieces straightaway and placed them in ice-cream bin bags, which were then covered in concrete.

She also told her neighbours that the noise coming from the premises was due to her 'new kind of ice cream machine'. The foul packages were then placed on a small trolley, transferred to the cellar and placed alongside the remains of her husband. But the strenuous work played havoc with her hands and being a woman who took pride in her appearance, booked a manicure to repair her damaged nails. As any stylish woman would do!

After disposing of Hinterberger's body, and not knowing what to do now, Estibaliz rang her brother and told him that Manfred Hinterberger had left her – leaving out the *small detail* she had murdered him.

But life goes on, and it was in the form of a new lover, Roland. A man who for the first time in her life fulfilled her expectations. At last, a truly perfect relationship. To cap her joy, one day in June 2011 she went to a gynaecologist and found that she was pregnant to her new lover.

In the meantime, two workmen repairing plumbing in the basement of her Schleckeria cafe came across the grisly remains and promptly notified the police.

As Estibaliz was telling Roland the happy news, there was a commotion in the street and a police car was now parked outside the cafe. Clearly something was amiss. She went down to investigate and was confronted by a neighbour who said, 'Have you heard the news, they say there are bodies in the cellar. They say that you killed them. Is it true?'

Realising the jig was up Estibaliz Carranza took off and a booked a flight to Paris and then onto Mexico. However, on reaching the airport she realised she could be tracked by police via her passport.

Now panicking, she took a taxi to Udine, Italy. An extraordinary decision, as the distance between Vienna and Udine is 459 kilometres (275 miles). A very long, expensive taxi trip!

Nevertheless, the two-months-pregnant Estibaliz was soon arrested and extradited back to Austria to stand trial. Her story was now front-page news, with her picture and the moniker, 'The Ice Cream Killer'.

On Monday 19 November 2012 the matter went on trial at the Supreme Court of Justice in Austria. Understandably, the trial attracted widespread media attention.

Estibaliz Carranza made a full confession to the court describing her husband as 'a violent and lazy bully' while her relationship to Hinterberger, her live-in boyfriend, was so poor she 'felt like she was in a prison … like my head was in a plastic bag.'

When she was arrested, Estibaliz Carrera was pregnant to another man, Roland. She gave birth to a baby boy in January 2012 and he was placed in the care of her parents in Barcelona. The couple were married in prison in March 2012.

She described her new husband as 'totally different' from her previous relationships saying, 'He is very gentle, the opposite of macho. He would not bring me into such a position.'

However, chief prosecutor, Petra Freh was not impressed, saying, 'This woman has two faces. She will try to play here the part of someone well-behaved, who would never do something like this. My task is to show you her other side. That she is a singularly cold-blooded and unscrupulous killer,' Adding ominously, 'Do not be fooled.'

The court wasn't, as numerous witnesses and seven experts were called to testify.

In a court ordered psychiatric assessment, Estibaliz Carranza was *deemed dangerous* and placed into a mental institution. A psychiatrist who examined her said she had 'a grave, comprehensive, multi-faceted personality disorder' – and could kill again.

She was subsequently sentenced to life in a secure mental health unit in Vienna.

Postscript:

In 2014 just prior to the release of her memoirs, Estibaliz Carranza was reported to have said, 'My actions have destroyed my life and dreams. I have a son and knowing how much he means to me has shown me how much I took away from two other mothers.' Adding, 'I would only want one wish – and that would be to change what happened.'

In January 2017 Estibaliz Carranza was considered still so dangerous that she was moved from her prison in Schwarzau, Austria, to a special centre in Asten near the city of Linz, 83 kilometres (50 miles) away.

Acknowledgements

My thanks to my publisher, Lesley Pagett, project editor, Liz Hardy and production director, Arlene Gippert for their skills and understanding, and to the excellent team at New Holland.

References & Further Reading

Chapter 1

Cassandra (1955) 'The woman who hangs this morning', *Daily Mirror,* 13 July 1955.

Ellis, Ruth (1955) *Woman's Sunday Mirror,* 26 June 26 3 July, 10 July and 17 July.

'Enemies' in *True Crime: Crimes of Passion* (2004) Janet Cave (editor) Time-Life, Caxton Publishing Group, London pp. 97–131.

Chapter 2

Kelleher, Michael (1998), *Murder Most Rare – The Female Serial Killer,* Praeger Press, Westport, CT.

Manners, Terry (1995), *Deadlier than the Male,* Pan Books (London).

Nash, Jay (1995), *Bloodletters and Bad Men* M. Evans & Company (NY).

Schechter, Harold & Everitt, David (1996), *The A–Z Encyclopaedia of Serial Killers,* Pocket Books (NY).

Chapter 3

'Dames and dirty rats', *The Sydney Morning Herald,* 26 May 2011.

'Never poisoned my husbands', *The Sydney Morning Herald,* 23 September 1952.

'Thallium murderess sentenced', *The Advertiser* (Adelaide), 24 September 1952.

'Woman sentenced to death', *The Sydney Morning Herald,* 24 September 1952.

'Woman sentenced to death for poisoning', *The Canberra Times,* 24 September 1952.

Chapter 4

'Kindly housewife won infamy as mass poisoner', *The Daily Telegraph,* 16 October 1953.

Supreme Court (New South Wales), depositions, 1953 (State Records New South Wales).

Court Reporting Office (New South Wales), Criminal Cases, 1953 (State Records New South Wales).

'Serial killer Caroline Grills served rat poison to her relatives', *The Daily Telegraph,* 15 February, 2019.

Chapter 5

'My mother was my husband's lover – Pretty wife's allegations in Bobby Lulham poisoning case', *The Argus* (Melbourne), 10 September 1953.

'Two divorce suits filed', *The Sydney Morning Herald,* 3 October 1955.

Chapter 6

Rule, Ann (1987), *Small Sacrifices,* New York, Signet Books. (This novel provides a more detailed version of this awful crime)

'Murderer's libel suit dismissed', *The Oregonian,* 18 January 1988.

'Reporter reflects on Diane Downs's murder case with new interviews on ABC's "20/20"', Bob Heye, KATU News, 23 March 2019.

'Woman finds peace after learning mother is convicted child killer Diane Downs', J. Taudte; K. Schiffman & E. Francis, ABC News, New York, 21 March 2019.

'Notorious convicted killer Diane Downs believes coronavirus swept through her prison, compares it to gothic horror story', *Pacific Northwest*, 17 April 2020.

Chapter 7

Spencer, Suzy (2015), *Breaking Point,* New York, Diversion Books. (This novel provides a more detailed version of this awful crime)

'Yates believed children doomed', C. Christian & L. Teachy, *Houston Chronicle*, 6 March 2002.

'Convictions overturned for mom who drowned 5 kids' NBC News, New York City, 6 January 2005.

'Doctor: I warned Andrea Yates not to have any more children', Fox News Channel, 7 July 2006.

'Yates not grossly psychotic before drownings Dietz testifies', D. Leron, *Houston Chronicle*, 13 July 2006.

'Fifteen years later, Andrea Yates case still resonates', B. Lewis, *Houston Chronicle*, 17 June 2016.

Chapter 8

'Fear as body found', *The Sydney Morning Herald*, 18 October 2007.

'Body in suitcase: police charge toddler's mother', *Sun Herald*, 21 October 2007.

'Mum refused bail over boy's death', *The Sydney Morning Herald*, 21 October 2007.

'The boy for whom help came too late', *The Sydney Morning Herald*, 22 October 2007.

'Hundreds attend Shillingsworth funeral' *The Australian*, 1 November 2007.

'Compassion plea as mother of boy in suitcase faces court' *The Sydney Morning Herald*, 13 December 2007.

'Body in suitcase: mum to stand trial', *The Sydney Morning Herald*, 28 October 2008.

'Mother pleads guilty to murder of son, 2' *The Sydney Morning Herald*, 18 August 2009.

'Mother gets 25 years jail for murder', *The Sydney Morning Herald*, 10 December 2009.

Chapter 9

Wilson, P.; Watson, R.; & Ralston, G. E. (1994), A Methadone maintenance in general practice: patients, workload, and outcomes. *British Medical Journal, 309*: 641–644.

Clarke, J. C; Milroy, C. M., & Forrest, A. R. W. (1995), 'Deaths from methadone use', *Journal of Clinical Forensic Medicine, 2*: 143–144.

Binchy, J. M.; Molyneux, E. M. & Manning, J. (1994), 'Accidental ingestion of methadone by children in Merseyside', *British Medical Journal, 308*: 1335–1336.

Arnow, R.; Sashi, P. D. & Woolley, P.V. (1972), 'Childhood poisoning: An unfortunate consequence of methadone availability', *Journal of the American Medical Association*, 219: 321–324.

Smailek, J. E.; Monforte, J. R.; Aronow, R. & Spitz, W. U. (1977), 'Methadone deaths in children: a continuing problem', *Journal of the American Medical Association, 238*: 2516–2517.

Geraghty, B.; Graham, E. A.; Logan, B. & Weiss, E. L. (1997), 'Methadone levels in breast milk', *Journal of Human Lactation,* 13(3): 227–230.

Wojnar-Horton, R. E.; Kristensen, J.; Yapp, H. P. et. al. (1997) 'Methadone distribution and excretion into breast milk of clients in a methadone maintenance programme', *British Journal of Clinical Pharmacology,* 44(6): 543–547.

McCarthy, J. J. & Posey, B. L. (2000), 'Methadone levels in human milk', *Journal of Human Lactation* 16(2): 115–120.

'Baby, aged 18 months, died of methadone overdose', *The Age,* 5 February 2003.

'Grandad's grief at drug death of a "happy little fellow"', *The Sydney Morning Herald,* 5 February 2003.

'Methadone overdose girl had 'regular user' levels', *The Daily Telegraph,* 23 January 2008.

'What the jury didn't know', *The Daily Telegraph,* 15 February 2008.

Allender, W. J. and Perl, J. (2013), 'Methadone Mothers', 51st Meeting & Conference of The International Association of Forensic Toxicologists, Funchal, Portugal, 2–6 September 2013.

Chapter 10

'Missing girl Kiesha Abrahams knew life's harsh cruelty', *The Daily Telegraph,* 4 August 2010.

'Kiesha Abrahams search called off', AAP, 8 August 2010.

'Mother, stepfather refused bail over murder', AAP, 22 April 2011.

'Police allege Kiesha was thrown against wall or bed', *The Sydney Morning Herald,* 10 June 2011.

'Kiesha stepdad "burnt and buried her body", Nine MSN News, 15 February 2013.

'Kiesha Weippeart's mother Kristi Ane Abrahams pleads guilty to her murder', ABC News, 17 June 2013.

'Mother finally admits: "I murdered Kiesha"', *The Sydney Morning Herald,* 18 June 2013.

'Kristi Abrahams jailed for at least 16 years over murder of daughter Kiesha Weippeart', *The Sydney Morning Herald,* 18 June 2013.

'Kristi Abrahams called "putrid dog" and told to "rot in hell" as she was sentenced to 16 years for the murder of "vulnerable and defenceless" Kiesha', The *Daily Telegraph,* 18 July 2013.

(This story has previously appeared in *The Expert Witness: A Second Dose,* by the author)

Chapter 11

Poisoning – Toxicology, Symptoms, Treatments (1986), J. M. Arena (editor) Charles C. Thomas, Publisher, Springfield, Ill., USA.

Baselt, R. C. and Cravey, R. H. (1977), 'A compendium of therapeutic and toxic concentrations of toxicologically significant drugs in human biofluids' *Journal of Analytical Toxicology,* 1: 81–103.

Felby, S.; Christensen, H. and Lund, A. (1974), 'Morphine concentrations in blood and organs in cases of fatal poisoning', *Forensic Science,* 3: 77–81.

Burt, J. M.; Kloss, J. & Apple, S. F. (2001), 'Postmortem blood free and total morphine concentrations in medical examiner cases', *Forensic Science,* 46(5): 1138–1142.

Jack, D. B. (1992), *Handbook of Clinical Pharmacokinetic Data,* Macmillan Publishers, pp. 4–5.

'Carer Kerry Forrest gave 84-year-old morphine overdose so she could use cash to build a house', *The Daily Telegraph,* 17 March 2014.

'Carer Kerry Forrest given effective life sentence for killing elderly man to feed her
gambling habit', *The Daily Telegraph*, 27 November 2014.
'Black Widow:Woman carer who poisoned war veteran before stealing his $300,000 and
blowing it on pokies told police he died "in his sleep"', *Daily Mail,* 4 June 2014.
'Carer Kerry Forrest almost certain to die in jail for defrauding, murdering William Anderson,
84', *The Sydney Morning Herald*, 27 November 2014.
(This story has previously appeared in *The Expert Witness: A Second Dose,* by the author)

Chapter 12
Australian Bureau of Statistics, Canberra, ACT (2006) for Aberdeen, New South Wales.
Disposition of Toxic Drugs and Chemicals in Man (2004), Randall Baselt (ed) 7th edition,
Biomedical Publications, California, pp. 488–489; 943–945.
'Therapeutic and Toxic Drug Concentrations' (1996), *TIAFT The Bulletin of the International
Association of Forensic Toxicologists,* vol. 26, no. 1, Supplement pp. 14, 21.
Allender, W. J. and Archer, A. W. (1984), 'Liquid chromatographic analysis of promethazine
and its major metabolites in human post-mortem material', *Journal of Forensic Science,*
29: 515–526.
'Slaying of a battler: Father's headless body found in house', *The Newcastle Herald,*
2 March 2000.
'Woman serves up her lover for dinner', *The Courier-Mail*, 19 October 2001.
'Knight loses appeal for skinning partner', *The Age,* 11 September 2006.
'The Black Knight: Katherine Knight stabbed her partner, skinned him and then tried to feed
him to his children', *The Daily Telegraph*, 5 May 2014.
Lee, Sandra (2002) *Beyond Bad – The Life and Crimes of Katherine Knight, Australia's Hannibal*
Bantam Books, Transworld Publishers.Sydney. (This publication provides a more detailed
account of this terrible crime.)
(This story has previously appeared in *The Expert Witness: A Second Dose* by the author)

Chapter 13
Disposition of Toxic Drugs and Chemicals in Man (2004), Randall Baselt (ed.), 7th Edition,
Biomedical Publications, California, pp. 252–254.
'Mentally ill woman Shamin Fernando lured her father to his death, court rules', *The Daily
Telegraph.* 16 December 2011.
'A father killed, a daughter lost', *The Sydney Morning Herald*, 6 April 2012.
'Retreat on gun laws destroyed my family', *The Sydney Morning Herald*, 28 April 2014.
(This story has previously appeared in *The Expert Witness: A Second Dose,* by the author)

Chapter 14
Textbook of Medical Physiology, A. C. Guyton & J. E. Hall, 10th edition, W. B. Saunders Co.,
Philadelphia, USA, pp. 884–898.
Disposition of Toxic Drugs and Chemicals in Man (2011), R. C. Baselt (ed.), 9th edition,
Biomedical Publications, California, pp. 845–848.
Velasco, C. A; Cole, H. S. and Camerini-Davalos, R. A. (1974), 'Radioimmunoassay of insulin,
with use of an immunosorbent', *Clinical Chemistry,* 20: 700–702.

Gallois, Y.; Caces, E.; Balkau, B. and D.E.S.I.R. Study Group (1996), 'Distribution of fasting serum insulin measured by enzyme immunoassay in an unselected population of 4,032 individuals', *Diabetes & Metabolism Journal,* 22: 427–431.

Birkinshaw, V. J.; Gurd, M. R.; Randall, S. S. et al. (1958), 'Investigation in a case of murder by insulin poisoning', *British Medical Journal,* 2: 463–468.

Bauman, W. A. & Yallow, R. S. (1981), 'Insulin as a lethal weapon', *Journal of Forensic Science,* 26: 594–598.

Haibach, H.; Dix, J. D. & Shah, J. H. (1987), 'Homicide by insulin administration', *Journal of Forensic Science,* 32: 208–216.

Iwase, H.; Kobayashi, M.; Nakajima, M. & Takatori, T. (2001), 'The ratio of insulin to C-peptide can be used to make a forensic diagnosis of exogenous insulin overdosage', *Forensic Science International,* 115: 123–127.

'Drugs, theft allegations, insulin injections: Nurse Megan Haines' history revealed', *The Sydney Morning Herald,* 5 November 2016.

'Megan Haines jailed for 27 years for murdering patients at Ballina nursing home', *The Sydney Morning Herald,* 16 December 2016.

'Ex-nurse challenges Ballina murder convictions', *Northern Star,* 26 October 2018.

'Nurse, 51, jailed for 36 years for murdering two people by deliberately giving them insulin overdoses loses appeal against her conviction', *Daily Mail,* 28 November 2018.

Chapter 15

Norton, Carla (1994), *Disturbed Ground: The True Story of a Diabolical Female Serial Killer,* W. Morrow & Co Publishers, New York.

Wood, William (2004), *The Bone Garden: The Sacramento Boarding-house Murders* IBooks, Publishers, New York. (These two novels provide a more detailed version of this awful crime.)

'Death house landlady got drugs from doctor prosecutors contend', *Los Angeles Times,* 25 March 1989.

'Dorothea Puente dies at 82; Boarding house operator who killed tenants', *Los Angeles Times,* 28 March 2011.

'Sacramento serial killer's home renovated, ready for visits', KCRA Channel 3, Sacramento, 29 August 2013.

Chapter 16

'Indian student Maulin Rathod killed in Australia', *Weekend Leader,* Canberra, 25 July 2018.

'The devil inside: What the jury was not told about teen killer's disturbing and violent history – as she's found guilty of manslaughter but not the murder of her internet date with a sex toy cord', *Daily Mail,* 19 December 2019.

'Accused did online "kill" searches before strangling man, court hears', *The Age,* 20 November 2019.

'Guilty verdict for "werewolf" woman who killed man she met on dating app', *The Age,* 19 December 2019.

'Sex toy strangler Jamie Lee Dolheguy could be out in three years', *The Courier-Mail,* 22 October 2020.

Chapter 17

'The nurse "who killed three babies"', *The Sun*, 22 November 1991.

'Nurse "only link to children's death"', *The Guardian*, 16 February 1993.

'Shadows of death fell across Ward 4', *The Times*, 18 May 1993.

'Killings fed a craving for attention', *The Times*, 18 May 1993.

'Serial killer nurse Allitt must serve 30 years', *The Guardian*, 6 December 2007.

'How "Angel of Death" Beverley Allitt was able to murder four babies and harm nine others',
   The Sun, 7 July 2019.

Chapter 18

'VA nurse charged with capital murder', APB News, 14 May 1999.

'Prosecutors seek death penalty for VA nurse', Associated Press, 25 May 1999.

'Murderous nurse escapes death penalty', ABC News, 26 March 2001.

'Nurse sentenced to life in prison for killing patients at hospital', Associated Press,
   27 March 2001.

(This story has previously appeared in *The Expert Witness: A Second Dose*, by the author)

Chapter 19

'Spurned woman "murdered ex-partner and poisoned his new lover with deadly Indian
   plant during reconciliation dinner"', *Daily Mail*, 7 January 2010.

'One minute we were eating, the next everything went dark: Curry-murder fiancée tells of
   the night her partner was poisoned', *Daily Mail*, 8 January 2010.

'Poison curry victim "was cheating on fiancée with woman who killed him"', *Daily Mail*,
   12 January 2010.

'Guilty of murder: Jilted woman who left ex-lover to die in agony after poisoning him with
   curry laced with deadly herb', *Daily Mail*, 11 February 2010.

'Jailed for life: Jilted woman who left ex-lover and his fiancée to die in agony after poisoning
   them with curry laced with deadly Indian aconite', *Daily Mail*, 11 February 2010.

Chapter 20

'Woman on trial for killing and sawing up husband and lover', AFP, 20 November 2012.

'Goidsargi Estibaliz Carranza Zabala pleads guilty to killing ex-husband, boyfriend in ice
   cream parlour', *Huffington Post*, 20 November 2012.

'"Ice killer" who chopped husband and lover up with chainsaw escapes jail', *Telegraph*,
   23 November 2012.

*Meine Zwei Leben: Die Wahre Geschichte der Eislady ('My Two Lives: The True Story of the Ice
   Lady')* (2014) co-written with Martina Prewein. Published in German by Edition A.
   (This publication provides a memoir account of these terrible crimes.)

www.ingramcontent.com/pod-product-compliance
Lightning Source LLC
Chambersburg PA
CBHW021228090426
42740CB00006B/440